SPORTS
INJURY CLINIC

SPORTS INJURY CLINIC

PELHAM BOOKS

PELHAM BOOKS

Published by the Penguin Group
27 Wrights Lane, London W8 5TZ
Viking Penguin Inc., 375 Hudson Street, New York 10014, USA
Penguin Books Australia Ltd, Ringwood, Victoria, Australia
Penguin Books Canada Ltd, 10 Alcorn Avenue, Toronto, Ontario, Canada M4V 3B2
Penguin Books (NZ) Ltd, 182–190 Wairau Road, Auckland 10, New Zealand

Penguin Books Ltd, Registered Offices: Harmondsworth, Middlesex, England

First published in Great Britain in July 1987
This edition reprinted in July 1994

Copyright © Sackville Design Group Ltd 1987

Typeset in Plantin by Optima Typographic Ltd, Wembley
Printed in England by Butler & Tanner, Frome and London

A CIP catalogue record for this book is available from the British Library

ISBN 0 7207 1753 1

CONTENTS

CONTRIBUTORS

Dr Malcolm Bottomley is Medical Director of the Sports Medicine for Doctors Distance Learning Course based at Bath University and has spent most of his professional life in general practice. He developed an interest in sports medicine while serving as Medical Officer at Ellesmere College in North Shropshire. He is currently a Medical Officer for the British Amateur Athletic Board.

Ian Burslem is General Manager for the International Footwear Division of Umbro Sportswear and is involved in the design and development of sports shoes. He has a degree in Sports Science from Liverpool Polytechnic and is a keen amateur sportsman.

Dr Seamus Dalton was a Research Fellow in Rheumatology at Addenbrooke's Hospital where he was involved in a sports injury clinic. He completed his specialist training in physiotherapy and rehabilitation medicine in Sydney, Australia, and returned to Sydney in 1987 to work as a consultant physician in a rehabilitation centre.

Paul McNaught-Davis is Principal Lecturer in Sports Science at Brighton University. He has particular research interest in

the aetiology of sports injury. He has also worked as a consultant editor on a book on health and fitness, and has created a new teaching unit called 'Developing Flexibility' for the National Coaching Foundation.

Graham Smith was the Head Physiotherapist/Director of The Football Association National Rehabilitation and Sports Injury Centre at Lilleshall National Sports Centre in Shropshire. He was previously involved in sports injuries as Honorary Physiotherapist to the British Amateur Athletic Board and as Physiotherapist to RAF and Combined Services Football Associations.

Dr Jacqueline Stordy is a Senior Lecturer in Nutrition and Food Science in the Department of Biochemistry at the University of Surrey. She has acted as nutritional consultant to various sports bodies, such as the Amateur Rowing Association, and has advised Olympic athletes during preparation for competition.

Brian Webster is District Superintendent Physiotherapist for East Birmingham Health Authority and has worked as a physiotherapist with the British Olympic Team.

INTRODUCTION

by J.B. King

Consultant Orthopaedic Surgeon, The London Hospital

At a time when we have the expectation of good health and sport for all, it is inevitable that the health care professionals and their resources are in danger of being overwhelmed by individuals who expect their doctors to have more and more training in sports medicine. It is therefore of growing importance that the sports participant becomes more and more involved in his or her fitness and preparation for sport. At the same time, recognition of the more common minor ailments – with some knowledge of their prevention and cure – will obviously take some of the burden off sports clinics. Having said that, however, it is essential that any major or prolonged problem is quickly referred to the appropriate professional.

Prevention is always better than treatment and it is for this reason that this book is compiled. The majority of injuries in sport are intrinsic, caused by overuse, abuse, misuse or disuse of the body by its owner. If individuals have an awareness of the mechanisms of sports injury, this will lead to its reduction.

As people return to or commence sport in later life, for example, they must have a graduated training programme to avoid undue stress on their cardiovascular system and limbs. As younger people compete more aggressively – be it against themselves or an opponent – training in risk avoidance is essential; this need for competition, incidentally, (whether in skill, weight or experience) is now established as a reducer of injury. Stress fractures – the fracture of bone by excessive use before adaptive strengthening takes place – are avoidable when the right precautions are taken.

It is conventional to divide injuries into major and minor. A minor injury is one preventable by common sense measures while the major injury comes about in a more unpredictable way, often because of an outside force. On that basis, this book will deal with the minor, preventable problems in terms of diet, clothing, preparation etc. Many sports injuries can be traced to some failure of coordination. This occurs at the beginning of the season when aspirations exceed abilities; at the end of tiring activity when coordination is lost from fatigue; in the first minutes of a game when stretching has not been performed and flexibility is not established; and after a previous injury, be it immediate or delayed, while muscle control remains incomplete.

All these situations are avoidable. It is sad that they occur so frequently. Sports injury clinics and doctors adequately trained in all aspects of sports medicine are still sufficiently rare that it is unjustifiable to make use of their time with easily preventable problems. Warm up, cool down, prepare yourself. That is what this book is about. It even addresses a problem first identified in the fifth and fourth centuries BC; that of sports nutrition. It is designed to help you to avoid the common pitfalls in technique and preparation, so as to avoid injuries and thereby prolong and enjoy your sport.

CHAPTER ONE

INJURY PREVENTION

Although it seems obvious, the importance of correct clothing and shoes in helping to prevent injuries in sports needs to be emphasised since it is something that many sportsmen and women tend to overlook. Coupled with this is the availability of orthotic devices which can help overcome certain physical abnormalities or weaknesses such as flat feet or unequal leg length: these can not only assist efficiency and performance but help a great deal in preventing injuries to which the individual would normally be prone. Different sports surfaces, too, can play a part in causing injuries and knowing how they produce varying degrees of friction and stiffness can help their avoidance.

So many sports injuries are unavoidable but those caused by wearing inappropriate gear are not. The aim in this section is to provide the sportsman with practical information about how he can help himself in this respect.

Clothing

This is very much an area of personal preference but the majority of guidelines are based on common sense.

- Clothing should be neither too loose nor too tight in fitting.
- Seams should be as flat and as smooth as possible to avoid rubbing.
- If training at night, ensure you can be seen. There is a wide range of clothing that incorporates night reflective material.
- Do not let fashion dictate the choice; the clothing must be functional.

One of the athlete's most important considerations when selecting clothing is that it must help maintain his body temperature within the limits that allow him to function efficiently. This will mean selecting clothing that insulates against low temperature and keeps body heat in to avoid hypothermia (over cooling), or conversely to allow the loss of body heat and the reduction of heat gain to guard against hyperthermia (over heating).

How heat is lost or gained

Heat is lost or gained in three main ways. Firstly, **radiation** is the transfer of heat from one object to another which are not in contact. Sportsmen normally lose heat in this way as they are at a higher temperature than their surroundings. Secondly, **conduction** is the transfer of heat from one object to another which are in contact. If air is continually moving past the body, the warmed air next to the body will be replaced by cooler air which in turn will be warmed and then removed. Thirdly, body heat is also lost through the **evaporation** of perspiration i.e. changing from a liquid to a gas. Heat is only lost when perspiration actually evaporates, so when the air close to the body becomes saturated this is not possible. However, if an air current passes over the body it can replace the saturated air with unsaturated air, thus allowing evaporation to take place.

Clothing for cold weather

In cold weather, it is important to have protection from the wind and to keep dry. Wind-proof garments will help as they reduce the amount of heat lost from evaporation but more importantly from conduction. Wet suits enable the athlete to keep dry and there has been a great advance in materials over the last few years. Materials are now available on the market that keep water out but allow the perspiration vapour to escape.

As a protection from cold, it is far better to wear a number of thinner layers than one layer of thicker material. A number of layers allow pockets of air to become trapped which acts as insulation. String vests are particularly good in this respect.

In cold weather approximately 35 percent

When running in cold weather conditions, you should wear warm, protective clothing. The woman runner wears warm tights and gloves for racing, whereas the man's hat prevents heat loss through the head while training.

of body heat is lost through the head. What is actually worn to combat this is personal preference, but a woollen hat that can be pulled down over the ears would seem a sensible choice. The hands are a part of the body that can give considerable discomfort in the cold. Light wool or cotton gloves are probably the best protection and it is surprising how quickly they do warm up.

Shorts and vest are the ideal clothing for running a marathon (right), but after the race (above) space-style thermal aluminium foil helps keep you warm, especially when your body temperature drops.

Clothing for hot weather

In hot weather, the aim is to lose body heat as quickly as possible. Clothing should not be tight fitting as this will reduce the amount of air able to circulate over the body and thus hinder loss through evaporation and conduction. Particularly important in hot environments is that athletes should be allowed to change perspiration-soaked clothing as often as possible. Once clothing is wet, it cannot absorb more perspiration, thus heat cannot be lost through evaporation.

Cotton and linen garments are superior to synthetic fibres in that they are absorbent, thus supporting the loss of body heat through evaporation. It is also more advantageous to wear light-coloured, shiny clothing as this reflects the heat while dull, dark clothing will absorb the heat.

Socks

Socks are an important consideration to any sportsman and clearly they should not be too big, as this can cause blisters, nor too tight, as they will restrict circulation. Cotton and wool are absorbent but hold perspiration while synthetic materials are long lasting, maintain better shape and help wipe perspiration away. The better socks, therefore, combine the advantages of both materials and cotton with a synthetic reinforcement is ideal.

Athletic supports

This is a much neglected part of the male sportsman's clothing and young athletes should be encouraged to wear an athletic support and develop the correct habits early. Ordinary briefs and sports shorts do not provide the necessary protection against movement when exercising, and so the individual is more likely to suffer from strains and tension in the groin area or even a rupture.

Women's underwear

Women should wear snug cotton briefs and above all, a bra which is supportive and comfortable. The straps should not interfere with sporting activity by falling off the shoulders and they should be wide enough so as to not dig into the shoulders. Any hooks and fasteners should not rub and the cups must fully support the breasts and prevent breast motion. The bra should be fairly lightweight and absorb perspiration (cotton or polycotton linings will help in this respect) and preferably a special sports bra, although the choice of these is somewhat limited in Great Britain and they are often difficult to find except in sports shops.

In many sports, like badminton (top), socks can help wick away perspiration and prevent friction between the shoe and the foot. Women athletes (left) can benefit from wearing a good support bra. There are many special sports bras on sale, some without chafening fasters and in specially absorbent stretch materials.

Protective pads and helmets are essential in dangerous sports like hockey (above) and speed skating (right). They help protect vulnerable parts of the body against injury and absorb single or multiple high-energy impacts.

Protective pads and helmets

It is worth mentioning the use of clothing to prevent injury through impacts with objects, with the ground or opposing players, e.g. in cricket, motor cycling, American football and ice hockey to name a few. One only has to look at American football, and even rugby, to a lesser extent, to see all the padding that is worn to protect players from impacts. Possibly the most advanced piece of protective clothing is the helmet. This should protect the head firstly, to prevent or reduce skull deformation, secondly, to reduce inter-cranial pressure which can damage the brain and thirdly, to protect against rotational motion. Most helmets have a fibreglass or plastic outer shell and an inner liner of either a crushable material to absorb a single high energy impact (as in equestrian sports or skiing) or a resilient material to absorb multiple impacts (as in American football or ice hockey).

Sports footwear

No section of clothing produces more debate between sportsmen than that of footwear. To understand fully the importance of footwear in injury prevention, it is necessary to have an idea of the biomechanics of running. The great advances in shoe design over the past decade or so owe a great deal to the research that has been conducted into running shoes. However, as the majority of sports involve running to some degree, these have also benefited from the findings.

Biomechanics of running

The foot is a complex structure and is constructed to absorb the initial impact upon landing. It then *pronates* (or turns inwards) to adjust to the surface and accept weight, after which it tightens up to prepare for the forward propulsion at take off.

When the foot is anatomically and biomechanically correct, it is the most efficient form of locomotion. The heel is narrow and has a fat pad around it that absorbs shock and then moves to the medial side (inside) of the foot which helps to reduce pronation. Shoes have the effect of increasing the amount of pronation in the vast majority of people for a number of reasons. First of all, the midsole material of shoes is softer than flesh and therefore allows more movement. Secondly, compared to running barefoot, the width of the heel in shoes is greater so that, upon landing, a greater lever is present to snap the foot into a pronated position. However, shoes are a necessity as the majority of surfaces are far from perfect. Let us now consider what happens when the foot makes contact with the ground.

Initial impact with the ground In running, the foot comes into contact with the ground from an angle and initial impact occurs for the vast majority of athletes on the outside edge of the sole. The angle of the foot at landing can vary from between 5-25 degrees to the vertical. In approximately 75-80 per cent of cases the initial contact occurs on the outside edge of the heel, and these athletes

Specialist lightweight running shoes will cushion and support your feet when running on hard road surfaces. They will make your running easier and more comfortable and help protect your feet and legs from injuries.

are classified as 'heel strikers' or 'rearfoot strikers'. The heel striker shows two force peaks, one at initial impact and another just before take off as the weight is transferred to the forefoot.

Between 15-20 percent of athletes land on the outside edge, but halfway down the length of shoe, giving the impression of landing flat footed. They are known as midfoot strikers and this type of contact is fairly effective in minimising impact. A rare group of athletes land on the forefoot and this usually occurs at high speeds.

Mid-stance phase After the initial impact, the mid-stance phase occurs. This is when pronation (or the foot's tendency to roll inward when striking the ground) takes

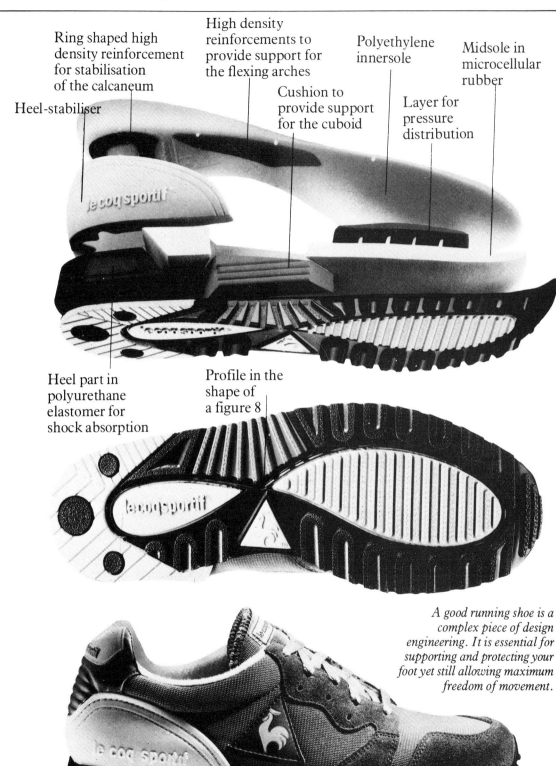

Ring shaped high
density reinforcement
for stabilisation
of the calcaneum

High density
reinforcements to
provide support for
the flexing arches

Polyethylene
innersole

Midsole in
microcellular
rubber

Heel-stabiliser

Cushion to
provide support
for the cuboid

Layer for
pressure
distribution

Heel part in
polyurethane
elastomer for
shock absorption

Profile in the
shape of
a figure 8

*A good running shoe is a
complex piece of design
engineering. It is essential for
supporting and protecting your
foot yet still allowing maximum
freedom of movement.*

Le Coq Sportif

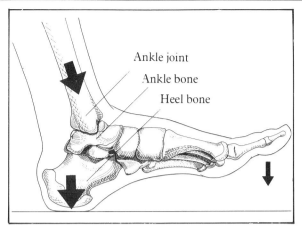

The shock absorption phase: the foot tilts slightly before striking the ground, causing it to land on the exterior side of the heel. This is heel-strike.

Ankle joint
Ankle bone
Heel bone

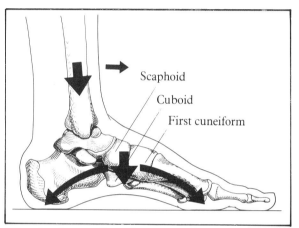

The forefoot strike phase: as the forefoot strikes the ground, the whole body weight is supported by the arch of the foot, making it tilt forwards.

Scaphoid
Cuboid
First cuneiform

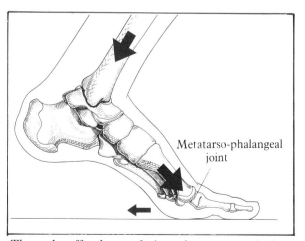

The take-off phase: during the metatarsal thrust propelling the body forwards, the heel lifts off the ground and the body weight shifts to the forefoot. You need to wear a supple support shoe.

Metatarso-phalangeal joint

place, some of which is both normal and necessary to absorb shock. However, too much pronation is one of the biggest causes of running injuries. As well as the amount of pronation, the rate (i.e. speed at which it occurs) is important.

Pronation problems

A foot that overpronates is loose and flexible, allowing excessive movement. It does not provide a rigid platform for take off, making it stressful and inefficient. Approximately 20-25 per cent of athletes overpronate and should look for a shoe with good motion control. Athletes who underpronate have a rigid foot which has an inability to absorb shock. They should look for a shoe with good shock-absorbing qualities and place little priority on motion control. The opposite of pronation is supination (hitting the ground on the inside of the foot and rolling outwards) but the number of athletes who supinate is insignificant.

Stability This is particularly important, during running, for overpronators, and also for sports which involve frequent changes of direction. A shoe in which stability is of importance should have a strong internal heel counter, preferably of plastic; an external heel support of some kind; a harder midsole material that allows less deformation during impact and, finally, a board-lasted construction which increases stability.

Cushioning This is the primary function of the midsole. However, there is an inverse relationship between cushioning and stability. The softer the midsole material, the greater amount of cushioning is obtained but it deforms and compresses so easily that stability is impaired. Shoes which improve cushioning while maintaining adequate control should have soft materials on the lateral side of the shoe to absorb impact, with harder materials on the medial side to provide support; various inserts such as gel and synthetic materials incorporated into the midsole; materials including Ethylene Vinyl Acetate (E.V.A), Polyurethane (P.U.) and Polyethylene (P.E.) used in combination with each other and, finally, shock-absorbing visco-elastic inserts.

Flexibility Inflexible shoes can cause injury because they place extra stress on muscle and ligaments. The foot flexes at an angle from the base of the big toe to the base of the little toe, not in a straight line across. Too many sports shoes are flexible, but in the wrong place. Soccer shoes with their plastic soles are often inflexible and could be improved in this respect.

Weight The weight of sports shoes is a much overrated factor with some sportsmen, particularly runners, many of whom believe that the lightest shoe is the best. This is not always the case as light shoes are often lacking in support.

Outsole grip and durability The outsole's main function is to provide grip and is discussed in greater detail in the sports surfaces section (page 19). A worn outsole can cause injuries through imbalance or through a lack of grip.

Uppers When buying sports shoes, always feel inside the uppers for lumps of material, hard edges or rough stitching. All are likely to cause blisters or cuts. The toe box should also be of sufficient depth to avoid blisters. One part of the upper which causes much controversy is the heel tab. A hard, inflexible heel tab can cause problems by digging into the tendon every time the athlete takes off. However, shoes may be modified to alleviate this by making two vertical slits through the tab either side of where the Achilles tendon is situated.

Orthotics and congenital physical reasons for injury

A significant number of sportsmen have congenital physical abnormalities or weaknesses which makes them prone to certain sports injuries and which also prevents them from achieving optimum running style. Fortunately, orthotic devices can now be

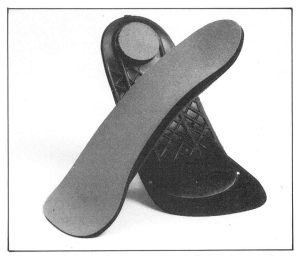

These orthotic arch supports are designed to balance and control the feet while running or just walking. They can be moulded in hot water to the foot shape.

incorporated into sports shoes to overcome such problems as flat feet, unequal leg length and a number of others.

Basically there are three types of orthotics – soft, semi-rigid and hard. Soft orthotics are primarily made from felt or foam and are useful when the abnormalities are not severe. Semi-rigid orthotics are usually made of soft, flexible plastic-type material and have the benefit of providing cushioning, dissipating weight more evenly and providing a better level of control. Hard orthotics are made of hard plastic or even steel and are not particularly suitable for athletes in sporting activity.

It is important that the orthotics are individually made and customised to your particular needs by experts. If this is not done, there is a risk of not correcting the abnormality or inducing another problem through over-correction.

Not all shoes are suitable for use with orthotics. Those which are must have an adequate heel counter height, as most orthotics will raise the foot to some degree. The heel counter should also be firm and have a snug fit to eliminate lateral or medial movement of the orthotic device. Most orthotics are also made to lie on a flat surface so the insock and any arch support must also be removed before fitting.

Flat foot (Pes planus)

Before looking at the difficulties associated with flat feet we should examine why the normal arch is beneficial. The arch is needed to adapt to new terrains and support body weight. However, modern man tends to walk on firm, even ground, with his feet protected by shoes with the result that the arches and supporting muscles are rarely used. The flat foot is the consequence.

The flat foot can be either mobile or rigid. The rigid flat foot is usually due to joint disease or muscle injury while the mobile flat foot can be caused by poor muscle tone. Flat feet allow the forces of impact to be dissipated because of the increased contact time with the ground. Also because they are hypermobile, they allow overpronation and can cause the associated injuries including plantar fasciitis, shin splints, chondromalacia, Achilles tendontis, ankle sprains and bunions.

The athlete with flat feet should look for a supportive shoe. An orthotic is frequently required and is often successful in alleviating the problem through a varus wedge, which raises the inside of the foot in relation to the outside, and some arch support.

High arched foot (Pess cavus)

The high arched foot can also be either mobile or rigid, although the rigid is more serious. The high arched foot does not pronate enough and consequently there is a lack of shock absorption. This predisposes the athlete to injuries including plantar fasciitis, stress fractures, iliotibial band syndrome, Achilles tendonitis, shin splints and calf muscle strains, which are similar to those for the flat foot, although the cause is different.

The athlete with a high arch needs to place good shock absorption as a prime objective and place less emphasis on motion control. An orthotic with a valgus wedge designed to pronate the foot is often helpful.

Bow legs (Genu varum)

Bow legs predisposes the athlete to overpronation. The legs are bowed i.e. curve inwards at the bottom, so they strike the ground at a greater angle than those with normal leg alignment. Therefore, for the feet to become flat on the ground, they need to pronate more. As a result, bow-legged people frequently suffer the injuries associated with severe pronation. An orthotic is helpful in this situation and usually consists of a varus wedge which raises the inside of the foot in relation to the outside.

Knock knees (Genu valgum)

Knock knees are characterised by the fact that when facing straight ahead the kneecaps are turned inward. This again causes the athlete to ovepronate and to be particularly prone to injuries such as chondromalacia and shin splints. Orthotics can help but professional or expert advice should be consulted regarding this complaint.

Unequal leg length

Unequal leg length (i.e. having one leg longer than the other) is a common occurence affecting a great many people and can be the cause of many sporting injuries. It is interesting to note that it is usually the longer leg that suffers the injury. To determine whether you have unequal leg lengths, a visit to a specialist is required. Once diagnosed, the use of a simple orthotic heel lift that corrects the imbalance is usually all that is needed for injury-free sports participation.

Different-sized feet

A great many people have a difference in size between their left and right foot, whether it is in length, girth or both. For the majority, the difference is so small that it causes no problems. For others it can be accommodated by variable-width lacing or the use of a thicker insock to take up room in one shoe. For a smaller group of people, the difference is so large that the only satisfactory way is to buy two pairs of different-sized shoes to get one pair that fits correctly.

Congenital female differences

There are differences between males and

females, both physical and physiological that predispose female athletes to suffer certain types of injury more frequently.

Pelvic differences Women possess a wider pelvis than men which causes the angle between the femur (thigh) and tibia (lower leg) to be greater for women than men. This puts women at a disadvantage when force of knee and hip extension is required and highlights the potential for injury at the knee, hip, pubic symphisis and sacrium/ilium junction. The increased angle means that the female leg points inwards towards the middle of the body and can cause a greater degree of pronation, with the related injuries.

Hormonal changes The mineral content of bone varies with the female menstrual cycle. If oestrogen levels are low, calcium is lost from the bones and they become weakened. This increases the risk of stress fractures.

During the pre-menstrual period, a hormone called relaxin is released which softens and stretches ligaments. This means joints become looser and are more vulnerable to shearing strains in particular. This helps to explain why women seem to be prone to lower back injuries in the pre-menstrual period.

Calf injuries Women's calves tend to be more susceptible to injury than men's for two reasons. Firstly, women tend to wear high-heeled shoes for normal day-to-day activity but when engaged in sport or exercise, the shoes are generally lower. This stretches the Achilles tendon – which attaches the calf muscles to the heel bone – and means it is more likely to suffer from an injury during activity. Secondly, women's calf muscles tend to tighten up during certain stages of menstruation, which has the effect of shortening the calf muscles and Achilles tendon, again making it more likely to suffer from injury. To avoid calf injuries, sportswomen should stretch the calf muscle adequately before activity and also ensure their sports shoes have adequate heel lift to release the strain on the tendon.

Foot structure Women's feet tend to be as broad at the forefoot as men's but narrower at the heel and with higher arches. Unisex shoes should therefore be avoided since they will be too big at the heel and so will not provide the necessary support and grip.

Sports surfaces

Different sports surfaces can cause a variety of sports injury depending, largely, on the degree of friction encountered and also on the hardness or stiffness of the surface.

Causes of injury – friction and stiffness

Friction is the force that acts between two bodies that are in contact with each other, i.e. the sole of the shoe and the floor. The frictional force acts to oppose motion. In sports, a fine balance is required between a high and low level of friction. A high level is needed to provide good traction and prevent slipping, while a lower level is needed to ensure the forces acting on the body are not above its physiological limit and likely to cause injury.

If there is person-to-surface contact, friction burns can be caused when the level of friction is not low enough. Needless to say, the presence of water dramatically alters the level of friction.

The sole of the sports shoe can alter the level of friction by the distribution and amount of tread and also the composition of the soling material. Of the three commonly used soling materials, it is generally accepted that rubber is the best, followed by P.U. (Polyurethane) and then P.V.C. (Poly Vinyl Chloride).

Stiffness is the ratio between an applied force and the deflection it causes i.e. the softness or hardness of the surface. Obviously, when an athlete falls on a surface, the softer it is the less likely he is to suffer an injury.

During running, stiffness is an important factor as the accumulated effects of running on hard surfaces can lead to a variety of injuries including stress fractures, shin splints and plantar fasciitis. In many cases, it is only possible to train or play on hard surfaces, so it is vital that shoes provide adequate cushioning.

Types of surfaces

Grass This is usually a soft surface which causes little injury as a direct result of impact. The frictional characteristics of grass vary, primarily with the influence of water.

The commonest games for which grass is used are field sports such as soccer and rugby. For these sports, studded boots are used to obtain grip. They do, however, have the disadvantage of becoming locked in the grass and the knee or ankle may be forced to move in an abnormal way liable to cause injury.

Artificial grass This covers a variety of surfaces, although most have the characteristics of a synthetic pile-top layer laid on a number of alternative bases. The frictional characteristics vary but are usually of a high level and this has been a reason why the number of joint injuries on this type of surface has been fairly high. A nylon top layer generally gives a higher level of friction than a polypropylene top layer. On artificial grass, the amount of friction that can be created is dependent upon the size of the total contact area between shoe and surface. A high level is obtained with a sole consisting of many small studs over its entire area.

Indoor carpet This type of surface consists of a synthetic thin-pile carpet laid on a solid base and .is particularly used for indoor tennis courts. It provides a high level of friction and when used with conventional footwear in the past produced a high level of injuries through sudden stopping and jarring. This led to the development of specialist indoor tennis shoes with a completely

Playing soccer on grass helps reduce the risk of injury even in severe tackles. However, if it is too lush and springy it can tire players out.

smooth outsole featuring no tread pattern, which reduces the level of friction. This is now a required type of footwear in many indoor tennis centres using carpet-type courts.

Concrete and asphalt Both these surfaces provide a good level of friction, although it is reduced when wet – which increases the likelihood of slipping. Neither concrete nor asphalt are recommended for sports which involve bodily contact, as the risk of injuries through jarring and abrasions is high. Both are hard surfaces, although asphalt does yield slightly more under pressure, and should be avoided for repeated training or running as the accumulated effects can lead to a number of injuries.

Timber Timber floors can be either laid on joints or directly on to a solid surface. When laid on joists, the resilience is greater as a springing effect is created compared to a solid base. Frictional characteristics are lower than concrete and asphalt and can cause slipping if highly waxed or polished.

Soft surfaces Throughout this section it has been highlighted that hard, stiff surfaces are liable to cause greater injuries than soft

Running on different surfaces and inclines puts various stresses on your body. Road running can be jarring to feet, leg and back muscles (left), and uphill running affects calf muscles and Achilles (above).

surfaces. However, extremely soft surfaces, such as sandy beaches, are far from ideal. A surface that sinks too much exaggerates any leg and foot imbalances that might already be present. A soft surface allows the heels to sink in causing Achilles tendon strain and also tends to push up the toes increasing the likelihood of plantar fascia strain.

Uneven surfaces This is particularly applicable to athletes engaged in frequent road running. The slant of the road can cause one leg to function as a longer leg leading to problems of leg-length inequality. The problem is easily remedied by continually swapping the side of the road used for running.

Hill running Running uphill places great strain on the calf muscles and Achilles tendon and increases the risk of injury to these structures. Before running uphill during training, a high amount of calf flexibility is needed.

Running downhill also causes problems. Shin splints can occur when muscles in front of the leg become overworked through trying to stop the forefoot from 'slapping down'. To prevent this, stretching and

Sports surfaces can be as varied as the rubber track (above left) and at the indoor track at Cosford (below left) and a wooden floor (above). When sportsmen change from one type of surface to another they should allow adequate time and practice to adjust.

strengthening of the muscles in the front of the leg and calf muscles should be undertaken. Overextending the leg can also cause ligament problems and irritation of the knee. To prevent this type of injury, the quadriceps should be strengthened.

Surface changes Changing from one type of surface to another can give rise to injury through the inability of the sportsmen to alter their style of play – as, for example when soccer players move from grass to artificial pitches or tennis players from a clay court to any indoor carpet surface. To illustrate the point, the tennis player accustomed to sliding into the shot on a clay court would find the level of friction far higher on an indoor carpet surface. Trying to slide into shots could cause injury to the joints and muscles. Experienced players, however, would alter their footwork accordingly.

Flexibility

Each joint in the body has its own range of movement. But the degree of movement will vary from joint to joint within an individual, and also between individuals. Most people, however sedentary, will have a naturally developed middle range of movement, sufficient for their everyday activities and only by *appropriate training* can this be improved towards the optimal, maximal flexibility, which should be the aim of all those who participate in sports activity.

Your personal flexibility around any particular joint will depend on a number of factors. These relate, firstly, to your anatomy and physiology and, secondly, to the type and intensity of your habitual activity. Some of these factors can be modified safely but others are limited by your particular genetic inheritance, and are modified only at the risk of actual tissue damage.

Improving your flexibility helps your sports performance level in general and, more specifically, helps you avoid injury. However, it is very important that you use sensible programmes of exercise aimed at improving flexibility safely.

Anatomy of flexibility

The 'frame' or supporting structure of the human body consists of a bony skeleton with various specialised hinges or joints, allowing independent and coordinated movement of the various parts. The skeleton is controlled by muscles, which pull on the bones to initiate movement, maintain stability, or restrict movement. For example, the muscles used when you kick a ball are the 'quads' – the primary movers of the lower leg. But the 'hamstrings' (tendons at the back of the knee) have to stretch as the leg extends and, after ball contact, they will reduce the speed of the limb by contracting, to help protect the knee joint. At the same time, the other leg is being stabilised by controlled counter-

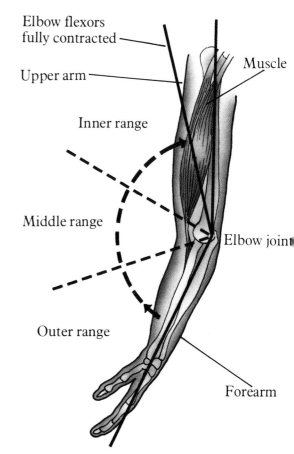

This illustration shows the conventional divisions of joint range, demonstrated here by the elbow joint. The range of movement results from the stretching of muscles and connective tissues.

balancing of the leg muscles around the ankle, knee and hip. To maintain your posture in anything but a lying-down position, muscles have to work and when a particular skill is being performed there will always be postural activity in various muscles around the body.

Natural limits to flexibility

If there is some outside application of a force, the joint has additional protection beyond that of the opposing pull of an 'antagonistic' muscle. Each joint has ligaments associated with it, and these are designed to restrict movement beyond the point at which damage may occur. The whole joint is surrounded by a capsule which, again, restricts the movement of the joint beyond its particular limits. Some joints have cartilage 'inserts' (knees, vertical column) which limit movement and act as shock absorbers. The length of these fibrous tissues (muscles, tendon attachments, ligaments, capsules) and the thickness of cartilaginous inserts will together form a natural limit to movement and flexibility. For example, as you bend backwards, the bones of the vertical column are squeezed together at its outer edge, and the discs of cartilage between these bones are also squeezed. What limits this movement, to a greater or lesser extent, is the 'inherited' thickness of these discs: thin discs allow less movement than thicker ones. If you try to go beyond your individual inherited limit, then actual damage is likely to occur. Although joint stability is maintained by connective tissue (ligaments, capsules etc.) and muscle tone (degree of tautness), these muscular elements may deteriorate with age, overuse or inactivity. As the muscles lose their youthful properties, the body relies even more heavily on the capsules and ligaments. If these have been over-stretched and damaged during years of physical activity, then joint stability can become a problem – nerves are trapped, joints degenerate, and we begin to suffer from sciatica, backache, knee soreness and so on.

Healthy connective tissue is designed to limit movement in a joint and if this tissue is damaged in the quest for fitness and/or improving flexibility, the bones may start to contact each other, resulting in further damage. Flexibility training has therefore to be done with care.

Physiology of flexibility

In order to understand how connective tissue works, we need to consider firstly, the neurophysiological attributes of tissue, and secondly, their biophysical properties.

When human connective tissue and muscle is stretched, there is an immediate relaying of sensory information to the central nervous system via the specialised nerve cells in the muscle, which are sensitive to change in tissue length. These sensory nerve trans-

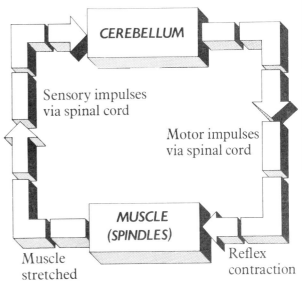

This shows the stretch reflex, illustrated by the knee jerk reflex when the patellar tendon is tapped causing a quadriceps contraction reflex.

missions initiate a *reflex* contraction of the muscles that have been stretched (the commonest example of this is the knee jerk). The faster and more ferocious the stretch, the stronger the contraction – which is designed to stop the muscle tissue from stretching. If you force the stretch, then actual tissue damage is likely.

Dynamic (bouncing) stretching exerts such a quick pull that the muscle, as pro-

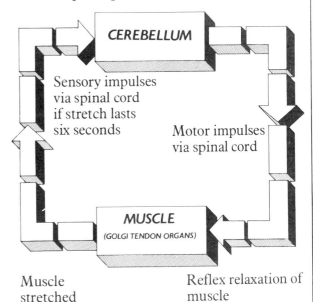

In the inverse stretch reflex, the impulses from the Golgi tendon organs over-ride the muscle spindles which relax reflexly after the initial contraction.

tection, acts against the movement; and if this protection is overcome, the result could be a sharp pull on the ligaments or capsules causing real damage. However, if a continuous rather than a jerky pull is put on the muscle, after about 6-10 seconds the resistance to stretching is reduced. This second reflex action is known as the *inverse stretch reflex*. It allows muscles to be pulled out to nearer their full length (often much longer than the apparent length – although the actual length of the muscles and ligaments does determine the limit to their actual range of movement).

Flexibility through 'plasticity'

When connective tissue is stretched, it becomes both elastic and plastic. In other words, if you pull it quickly it will stretch and then return to its original length, like a rubber band. If, however, you apply and hold a steady pull on the tissue, there is a continuing stretching out – beyond that elastic limit.

It has been shown that this plasticity is best achieved by using low force and a long duration, while keeping the tissue hot. In the training situation, this means that you need to be warmed through thoroughly, use minimum force, and then hold the stretch at its limit for an extended period. It is this *plastic* stretching which promotes the real improvement in tissue length, therefore improving flexibility. So neurophysiologically, a slow, steady stretch – overriding the stretch reflex safely and achieving an effective pull on the tissues – can improve flexibility without doing harm.

Tension

Tension obviously affects the muscles' capacity for flexibility in that the tenser the muscle is, the more the resistance to the stretch. Encouraging relaxation is therefore an important part of good flexibility training which, of course, should never become competitive, since this usually increases tension, and so limits improvement.

Respecting natural limits

As has been pointed out, some aspects of tissue structure and function cannot be safely altered. Because the anatomy of the human body has these important inbuilt factors, a golden rule of flexibility training must be to respect these natural limits. Not everyone, however much they train, can safely reach the extremes of flexibility seen, for example, among top gymnasts. It is very worrying that many gymnastics clubs and other such groups seem to expect all their pupils to achieve similar joint flexibility, without taking any account of their individual differences. Many doctors and physiotherapists involved in sport have already voiced these fears, in terms of long-

This shows the position of the proprioceptors in the muscle during the stretch and inverse stretch reflexes (both illustrated on page 23).

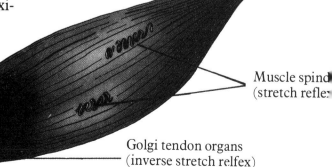

Muscle fibres

Tendon

Muscle spindle
(stretch reflex)

Golgi tendon organs
(inverse stretch relfex)

term effects that may not be apparent until some years after. Of particular concern are the pre-pubescent girls and boys who are exploiting the pliability of a semi-mature skeleton to increase flexibility. They are, by their actions, endangering the skeletal system at maturity – which may have serious implications.

Flexibility for sports injury prevention

There are two types of flexibility: firstly *static* flexibility, which is the limit to which a joint can be moved passively with the aid of, say, body weight or an apparatus; and second, *dynamic* flexibility, which is the range through which you can purposely move the joint by using the muscles around it. For example, a gymnast doing the splits in the normal way is using static or passive flexibility. Her weight, bearing down on the limbs, is pushing them to their limit. If the gymnast were to lie on the floor and pull her legs into the same position, using the leg muscles, she would be using dynamic flexibility at the hip joint.

In most sports, it is dynamic flexibility that is important for the performing of skills. In golf, for example, the bigger the dynamic swing, the faster the club head can be moved – and the further the ball can go. Static flexibility will not help the power stroke, although it may help in other situations. Imagine, for example, that your leg is forced towards its limit by a tackle in football. A good degree of static flexibility in this case may allow the limb to be pushed beyond its dynamic range, but without being damaged.

Although you may normally only use the mid-range of flexibility in any skill, if strength and muscle control has been developed over a wide range – i.e. you have improved your dynamic flexibility – then you have a greater safety margin. You can protect the joint actively because you can bring muscles to bear, even at the extremes of your flexibility range.

Flexibility training is important for the joints in another way: joint surfaces are not supplied with blood, but get their nutrients from a thick lubricating fluid produced by the synovial membranes. When joints are worked only over a limited range, unused surfaces of the joint are less well lubricated and there will be a steady deterioration, followed by restriction of movement. So flexibility exercises help keep the joints in good working order, and reduce the rate of tissue degeneration. At the same time, lubricating oil is supplied to the skeletal hinges, and so keeps them from getting 'rusted up', creaky and difficult to move.

A sensible programme of flexibility training can therefore protect your joints from injury in sport. First, by improving the static flexibility, you have a safety margin into which the limb can be pushed beyond your dynamic range without damage. Second, by improving the dynamic range, the joint can bring in a wider range of muscles to bear against a potentially damaging force.

Good flexibility can also help to increase your skill levels in your particular sport. For example, speed over the ground is dependent on the speed of the foot-strike and the degree of hip flexibility, among other things. If you can run faster, then what was an even chance can become slightly weighted in your favour.

There is one final advantage to flexibility development. By performing all this slow stretching activity in a non-competitive, warm and relaxed environment, you are able to concentrate on your muscles and become aware of them in a very important way. This probably improves the coordination of one muscle with another, makes the brain better-reacting to sensory nerve impulses from the muscles, and really begins to tune the mind and body – and that *must* be good for injury prevention.

Programme for flexibility improvement

There are some important general points which should be taken into consideration for flexibility training. You can and should do as much stretching as you like but it is essential that you obey the following simple rules.

- Always be very well warmed up before you start, and if necessary warm up *between* flexibility exercises as well.
- Stretch each muscle in turn by *slowly* going towards your limit.
- *Hold* the stretch at the point of resistance: *do not* go as far as *pain*.

- Keep relaxed, breathe all the while and do *not try to compete* with anyone.
- Choose exercises where you have to use your muscles to get to the stretched position and *not* the body weight.
- *Never 'bounce' any joint.*
- Every day, for 10 to 20 minutes, is better than exercising twice a week for an hour. An hour every day would be better still.
- Make sure you balance your flexibility training, so all muscles get a good stretch.

- Do not expect very quick results. Flexibility takes longer to improve – but also takes longer to lose – than other aspects of fitness.
- If you are hyper-mobile (i.e. very, very flexible – sometimes called 'double-jointed') *do not* do any flexibility exercises, but try to increase the strength of the muscles near their outer limits.
- When doing flexibility exercises, you should also try to improve strength over the same range of movement.

Flexibility exercises

Try some of the exercises below for good stretches. Again, with each one you must use a slow stretch until you feel resistance, and then hold the stretch for 10 seconds. As you improve, this can go up to 30 seconds or more. Repeat the stretch two or three times before moving to the next one.

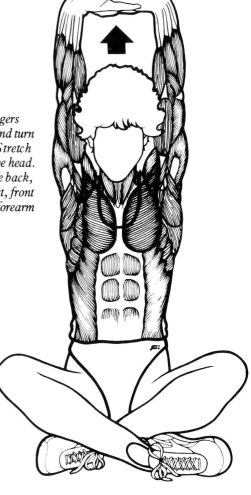

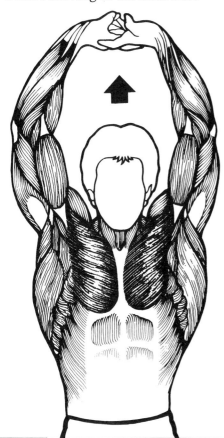

Interlock your fingers above your head and turn palms upwards. Stretch arms up high above head. You should feel the back, rear shoulder, chest, front of upper arm and forearm muscles all being stretched.

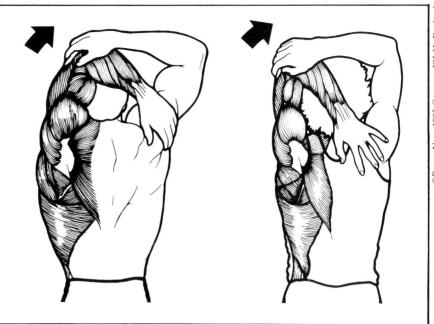

With arms overhead, gently pull the elbow behind your head with the opposite hand. Hold when you reach a comfortable stretch in the rear shoulder and upper back muscles. Repeat to the other side.

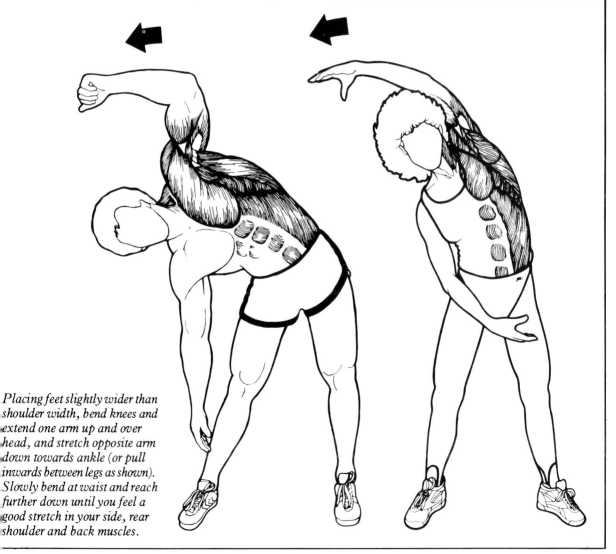

Placing feet slightly wider than shoulder width, bend knees and extend one arm up and over head, and stretch opposite arm down towards ankle (or pull inwards between legs as shown). Slowly bend at waist and reach further down until you feel a good stretch in your side, rear shoulder and back muscles.

©Bruce Algra 1985. Courtesy ISLM, England.

Grasp your hands behind your back and lift arms up slowly until you feel a stretch in the chest, front shoulders and front of the upper arms.

4

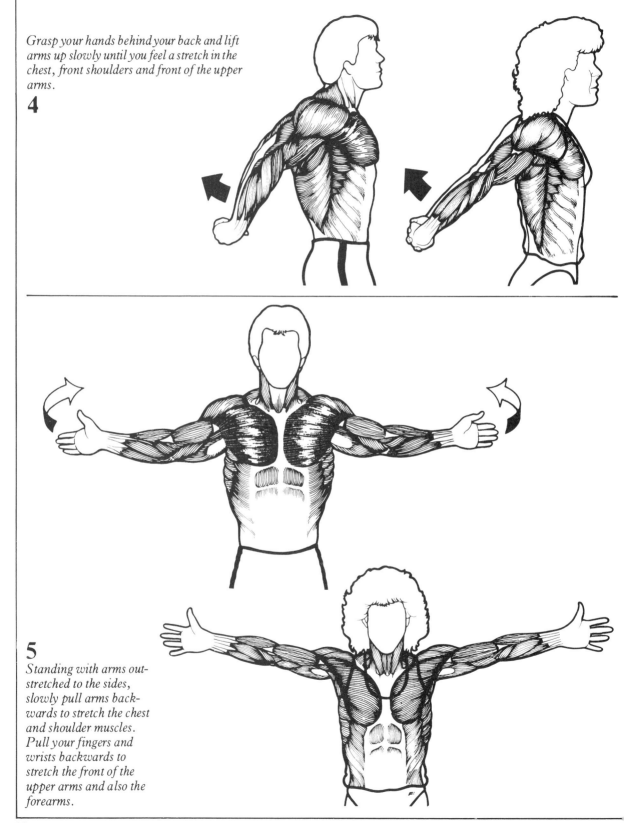

5

Standing with arms out-stretched to the sides, slowly pull arms back-wards to stretch the chest and shoulder muscles. Pull your fingers and wrists backwards to stretch the front of the upper arms and also the forearms.

Sit with your right leg crossed over your outstretched left leg with your right arm behind for support and left hand resting on right knee. Slowly turn your head to the right over your right shoulder as you pull your right knee in the opposite direction. Alternatively, support your body with both hands flat on the floor to the right of your right knee. Feel the stretch in your hip, side and upper back. Repeat to the left.

6

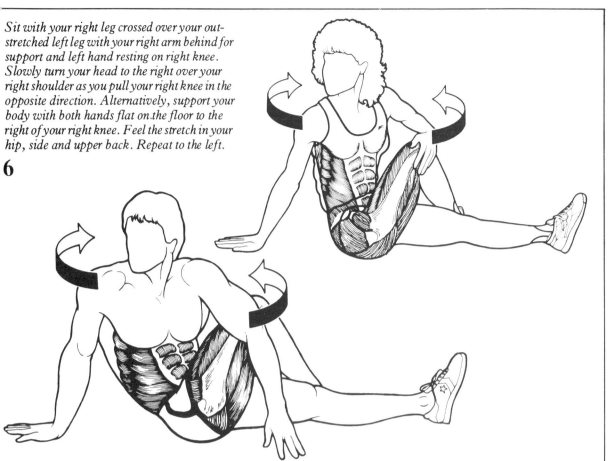

Sit with legs straight, knees locked-out and ankles flexed. Bend forwards from the hips as far as possible towards your toes until you reach your stretch position (do not bounce or jerk). Hold the position and then relax. You will feel some tightness just behind the knee joint, in the upper calf and in the lower back. You do not have to touch your toes to stretch your hamstring muscles effectively.

7

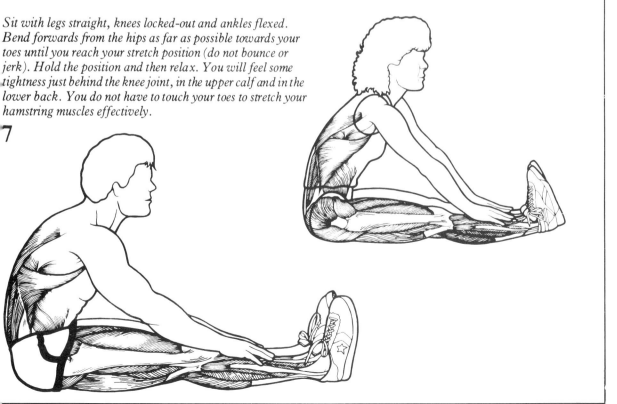

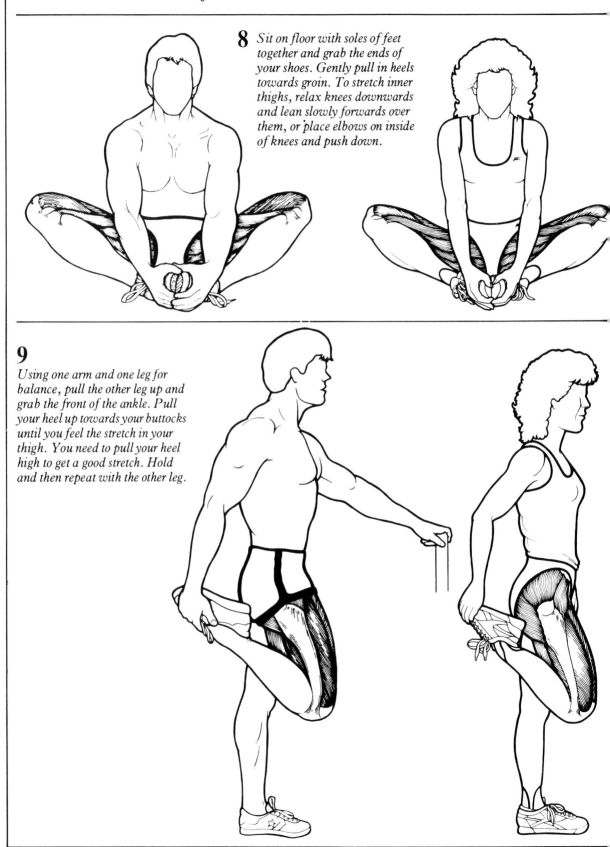

8 *Sit on floor with soles of feet together and grab the ends of your shoes. Gently pull in heels towards groin. To stretch inner thighs, relax knees downwards and lean slowly forwards over them, or place elbows on inside of knees and push down.*

9

Using one arm and one leg for balance, pull the other leg up and grab the front of the ankle. Pull your heel up towards your buttocks until you feel the stretch in your thigh. You need to pull your heel high to get a good stretch. Hold and then repeat with the other leg.

Stand with feet shoulder width apart, knees flexed and toes pointing straight ahead. Bend forwards at the hips and let your arms relax down as far as feels comfortable. Aim to touch your toes eventually. Feel the stretch in your hamstrings, calf muscles and lower back. Stretch gently and smoothly _ do not bounce or move jerkily.

10

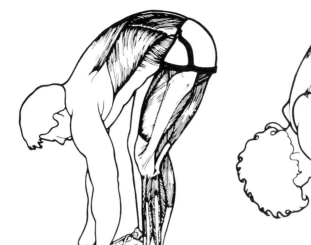

© Bruce Algra 1985. Courtesy I.S.I.M. England.

11 Kneel with feet in direct alignment to knees and arms placed behind for support. Slowly and smoothly lean back to stretch thigh muscles.

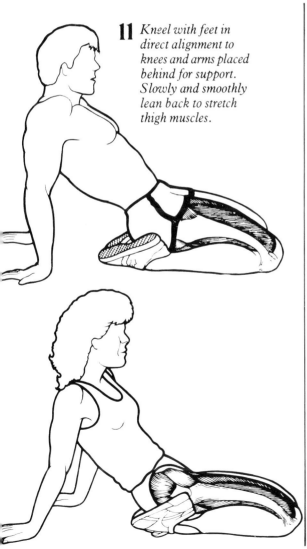

12

Stand facing a wall, one leg behind the other and locked-out. Lean on it with hands. Bend elbows and lean forwards to touch with head, keeping feet flat on floor. Or stand with one foot 2-3 feet in front of other and turn toes of back foot in slightly. With both feet flat on floor, slowly bend knee of front leg to stretch calf muscles. Repeat with other leg.

Stress and injury in sport

All individuals, and particularly sportsmen, are subjected to a certain amount of stress and almost everyone has experienced those feelings of excitement and exhilaration before and during a competitive match or game, as well as the apprehension and frustration that takes over when things are going badly. All sportsmen know that their psychological attitude to the game is just as important as their physiological fitness for the sport; you need to be in the right frame of mind to play well. If you are not, not only will your performance suffer but you may also be more susceptible to injury.

What is stress?

Stress occurs when we are unable to cope with the demands made upon us. These can be imposed by the individual himself, when he sets up goals and needs he wishes to satisfy. But external demands can also be made by the situations in which we find ourselves, or by other people. The important thing in terms of stress is our *perception* of the demands and of our ability to cope. If we do not think a situation is particularly demanding, then we do not feel stressed until we are unable to cope with it – but only if coping is *important* to us. So it is our perception of demand, ability to cope and the importance of coping which dictate when stress occurs.

How we respond to stress

People respond to stress in psychological, physiological and behavioural ways. Psychologically, we tend to describe our feelings emotionally – for example, by feeling worried, frustrated, apprehensive or even anxious. At the same time, we experience physiological sensations associated with the emotional feelings. These may include increased heart rate, muscular tension, sweating and 'butterflies in the stomach'. We then act in such a way that enables us to cope with the situation to a greater or lesser degree. If we do not cope adequately – or at all – the emotional and physical signs of stress will stay with us and, if unresolved over long periods of time, can be the cause of illness or disorders like depression and heart disease.

Good and bad stress

Not all stress is bad. In fact, some measure of 'positive' stress is essential for the sportsman. This occurs when we are faced with a demanding or challenging situation which requires us to extend our proven capabilities or to take a calculated risk in order to succeed. Having done so and 'coped successfully', we have an overwhelming feeling of satisfaction which is one of the rewards of sport. And without such situations, the challenge and excitement of the game would be lost. However, the difference between good and bad stress is a narrow one, as anyone who has watched the finals of, say, a tennis or soccer match knows. It is only when things begin to go wrong that we lose confidence, feel unable to cope and at worst experience apprehension and fear. Both good and bad stress can result in injuries.

Injuries caused by stress

Sports injuries frequently occur when we either over- or under-estimate our actual abilities. When under a lot of bad or negative stress, the individual's judgement and decision-making is impaired. This kind of stress also has a physically debilitating effect, which is why losers look and feel more tired and worried than those who are winning. In a high-risk sport such as rugby, an incorrect decision to tackle an opponent can, of course, cause injury to both the individual and the other player.

Positive stress also has its dangers. In accepting a challenge and overcoming it successfully, many sportsmen push themselves beyond their physical capabilities. Only later do they realise they have sustained an injury.

Stress caused by injuries

When a sportsman is injured, the amount of stress he is likely to suffer depends not only on the seriousness of the injury but also on his emotional response to it, which usually includes anger and frustration and sometimes apprehension and fear. Generally, he is concerned with how quickly he will recover and be able to continue training and competing – and whether his performance will suffer because of the injury. Basically, sportsmen who are injured need help in adjusting mentally to the injury and in planning programmes to aid recovery. Those who are severely injured and cannot continue their sports activity need particular help in coming to terms with their loss and may go through periods of deep depression before they can properly face reality.

Techniques for dealing with stress

How can the sportsman deal with the stress associated with injury? First of all, he must develop a positive attitude towards recovery, look upon the injury as a challenge to be met, and set realistic goals in relation to rehabilitation. This must be done in consultation with the coach and the doctors, specialists and physiotherapists dealing with the injury. These experts will know the priorities and what is possible and realistic in setting short term and long term goals. It is important for the sportsman to know when he can expect to return to competition. Let us say that the total recovery and return to fitness will take three months. The long term goals should be decided first, then the intermediate goals for the intervening weeks and months and it is important that the whole programme is put down in writing so that the patient knows precisely what he is doing and why. As he works his way through the rehabilitation programme, the goals should be reassessed and modified according to his progress.

Mental preparation in training

Today, many sportsmen use mental preparation as part of their total training programme and consider it just as important as physical preparation. Part of mental preparation is learning to mentally and physically relax, using one of the available relaxation techniques. When the individual has learned to relax and put himself into an altered state of consciousness, he is then able to develop the techniques of concentration, visualisation and mental rehearsal. Using these techniques, it is possible to reach the correct level of arousal and what is termed the 'ideal performing state'.

Visualisation and mental rehearsal

Relaxation techniques aid physical and mental recovery after hard training sessions or competition and they can also assist recovery from injury. When a sportsman is injured, he is usually unable to train or practise the skills of his sport. One of the best ways of overcoming this problem is to use visualisation and mental rehearsal. First, the individual puts himself into a relaxed state and goes back in time to his best performance. He then plays it through, visualising and mentally rehearsing his performance and feeling all the sensations associated with that particular game or match. By doing this regularly, he retains or even improves the mental programmes or skills he has learned by keeping them active. Best performances are usually associated with the ideal performing state and this is usually associated with feelings of ease of performance, everything appearing to happen in slow motion, and sometimes the feeling that the sportsman is watching himself play. By mentally rehearsing and visualising a past best performance, he is able to retain the sensations or feelings of the ideal performing state.

These techniques should be an essential part of all sports training programmes. In addition, it is important that the programme is carefully planned in consultation with the sportsman and that the goals set are realistic. Meeting these goals in training and competition builds up confidence and motivates the sportsman even further.

CHAPTER TWO

THE SPORTS BODY

How the sports body works

The human body responds to exercise, training and sports activity in a highly complex way which involves co-ordinated action between the brain and the muscles, the raw material of movement. Precisely how the brain sends messages to muscles to initiate movement is fully explained in text books on neurophysiology and athletes and coaches seriously involved in sports activities will want to make a detailed study of these intricate mechanisms. The average sportsman, however, does need to know generally how muscles, bones, tendons and tissues interact so that in training and exercise he or she knows how injuries can occur and, more to the point, how they can be prevented.

What are muscles

Muscles are a collection of specialised cells that have the ability to change their length by contracting or expanding and they can also develop tension. Essentially, a muscle consists of thousands of fibres bound together by slightly elastic connective tissue. Each fibre is kept separate by connective tissue called the *endemysium* and each bundle of fibres is covered by further connective tissue called the *perimysium*. Keeping the whole muscle encased and separate from its surroundings is another tissue, the *epimysium*. These muscle fibres, blood vessels and connective tissues can all be stretched or torn during exercise or sports activity which is why warming up is so important since it loosens these tissues, making them more elastic and less liable to tear.

Tendons

These link muscles to bone and each tendon consists of bands of very strong and only slightly elastic collagen fibres. The fibres are joined at the bone end by way of widespread attachments which almost form part of the bone itself. At the muscle end, the tendon

The male muscular and skeletal system

1 Frontalis	24 Sternum	48 Phalanges
2 Trapezius	25 Humerus	49 Axis
3 Deltoid	26 Costal cartilage	50 Ilium
4 Pectoralis major	27 12th rib	51 Coccyx
5 Triceps brachii	28 Ulna	52 Adductor magr
6 Latissimus dorsi	29 Sacrum	53 Semitendinosu
7 Biceps brachii	30 Radius	54 Sartorius
8 Brachioradialis	31 Pelvic inlet	55 Trapezius
9 Rectus abdominis	32 Ischium	56 Supraspinatus
10 Pectineus	33 Pubis	57 Deltoid
11 Rectus femoris	34 Carpals	58 Infraspinatus
12 Vastus lateralis	35 Metacarpals	59 Teres minor
13 Peroneus longus	36 Phalanges	60 Teres major
14 Peroneus brevis	37 Adductor longus	61 Latissimus dor
15 Tibialis anterior	38 Gracilis	62 Gluteus mediu
16 Extensor	39 Sartorius	63 Gluteus maxim
digitorum longus	40 Femur	64 Iliotibial tract
17 Sphenoid	41 Vastus lateralis	65 Biceps femoris
18 Mandible	42 Patella	66 Gastrocnemius
19 Hyoid bone	43 Tibia	67 Soleus
20 Cervical column	44 Soleus	
21 1st rib	45 Fibula	
22 Clavicle	46 Tarsals	
23 Scapula	47 Metatarsals	

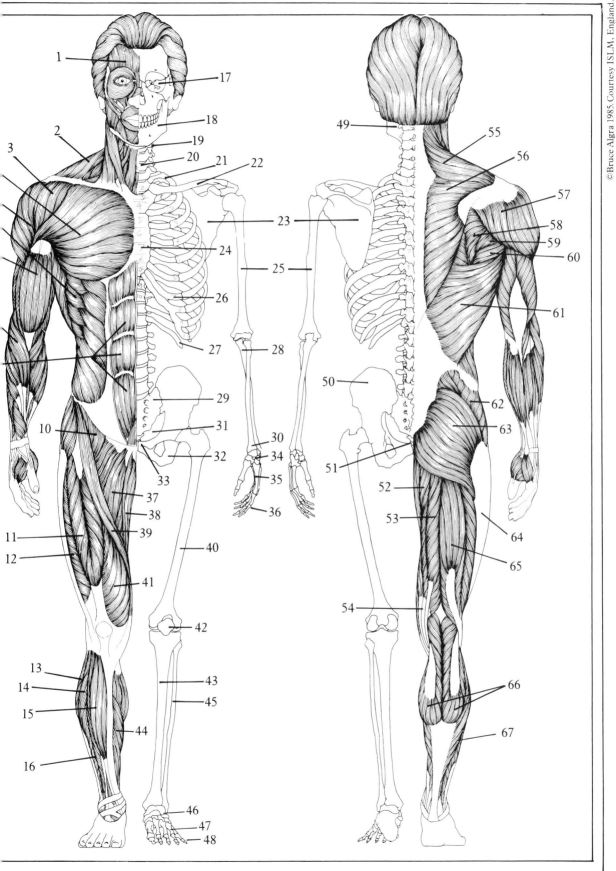

merges into the connecting tissue surrounding the muscle. The tendon is capable of withstanding considerable stresses but, like the muscles, it may stretch or tear or become inflamed, resulting in pain and injury.

Skeletal structure

The muscles would be entirely useless in the body without the presence of bones. The bones in the limbs are mainly long bones such as the femur, tibia, humerus and ulna. Where fine movement is required such as in the wrist and ankle, there are a number of small bones. The bones are held to each other by fibrous tissues called *ligaments* and where the bones move together at a joint there is the articulating *cartilage*, a tough polythene-like material, the thickness of which varies from individual to individual. To help prevent friction, the joints are encased in a capsule which is filled with the lubricating synovial fluid which also supplies nourishment to the cartilages. Cartilages and ligaments do get damaged in sports activity with sometimes more serious results than, say, a broken bone since the repair of these connecting and protective tissues is often difficult. The bones themselves, as well as being subject to breaks or fractures, can also be dislocated, as frequently happens with the shoulder.

Well-tuned body

Although there is potential for serious injury in sports activity, most are in fact minor aches and strains, many of which the sportsman can treat himself. However, each part of the system must be kept in tune for the body to work well and it is through exercise and training that this can be accomplished. Without this, serious injury can and does occur. Sports injuries are set out below according to the part of the body involved, which allows the individual to refer quickly to the area of his or her problem. Suggestions for treatment are given but it must be firmly stated that if the sportsman has any doubt about the nature or seriousness of his injury, a doctor *must* be consulted; only minor injuries should be treated without professional advice.

For basic treatments (rest, ice, compression and elevation) and for abrasions, infections, cramp etc, see Chapter 3 on *Self-Help*, pages 82-95

Head injuries

Concussion and unconsciousness ('knockouts')

Head injuries are most common in horse-riding, boxing, rugby and Alpine skiing, or in football where there may be a collision of heads. The unconscious person should be placed on his side (provided there is *no* evidence of neck injury) and examined to ensure that he is breathing normally and that the mouth is cleared of any obstruction such as mud, dentures or a mouthguard. The head should be tilted gently backwards and the jaw pulled forward to allow free passage of air to flow into the lungs. A doctor must be consulted.

After a blow to the head, a person may be confused, disorientated and unable to answer simple questions. This is a form of concussion and if on the sports field, the player should be removed from play and kept under observation until examined by a doctor.

Treatment
This must be administered by a doctor and return to sport should be closely controlled, as repeated episodes of concussion can cause minor degrees of brain damage. An extreme example of this is the 'punch-drunk' boxer. It is reasonable to follow these guidelines: a significant episode of concussion requires

three-weeks rest from contact sports; if there are two to three episodes during one season, the person should cease playing for the rest of that season; more than five episodes and the person should be advised to give up the particular sport. A period of unconsciousness requires one to two months off sport, depending on the duration of unconsciousness at the time of injury. Suitable headgear is available as a preventative measure in a number of sports (cricket, boxing, horse-riding, rugby, cycling, American football and ice hockey).

Eye injuries

Direct injuries to the eye can be serious, especially in the case of squash where the ball fits exactly into the eye socket. Even minor scratches to the eye surface carry a high risk of infection. Any eye injury in which there has been direct contact with the eyeball, particularly if there is blurring of vision, requires medical attention.

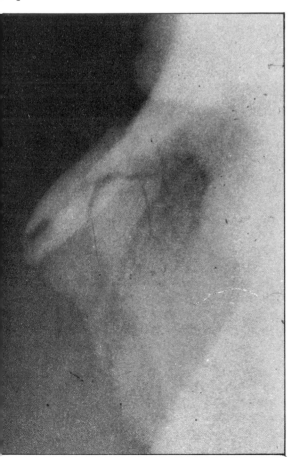

Cauliflower ear

This occurs as a result of bleeding into the outer ear which causes swelling. It is common in rugby forwards involved in scrummaging.

Treatment
Early treatment with ice and compression is essential to prevent the 'cauliflower' from developing. Needle aspiration of the blood can be carried out by a doctor, if the swelling does not settle with first aid.

Nose injuries

Nosebleeds are common in many sports and bleeding usually stops in about 15 minutes.

Treatment
They are best treated by sitting upright, pinching firmly on the nose and applying cold for about ten minutes. If bleeding has not stopped after 30 minutes or if a fracture is suspected (i.e. if there is a deformity of the nose), see a doctor immediately.

Dental injuries

Injuries to the mouth can cause loosening or breakage of teeth. The importance of wearing a well-fitting mouthguard cannot be over-emphasised in contact sports such as rugby, boxing or even hockey. Dental help should be sought as soon as possible.

Injuries to the cheekbone

A direct blow on the cheekbone can cause a facial fracture. This should be suspected if there is tenderness and swelling over the cheekbone and especially if chewing is painful or if the shape of the bone appears altered.

Treatment
Seek medical attention immediately.

X-ray of a nasal bone fracture. Nasal fractures occur in many contact sports such as boxing and rugby. Bone deformity or excessive bleeding are symptoms.

Injuries to the lower jaw (*mandible*)

A fractured jaw should be suspected after a direct blow if there is pain on opening or closing the mouth (especially on clenching the teeth), if there is bleeding into the mouth, if there is marked local tenderness (always check in front of the ear) or if the teeth seem to be out of alignment.

Treatment
Seek medical attention immediately.

X-ray showing a fractured lower jaw. This is usually the result of direct force, such as a heavy blow to the jaw.

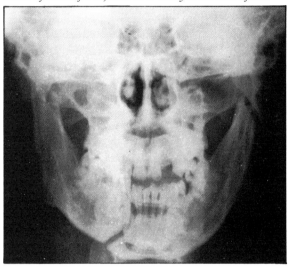

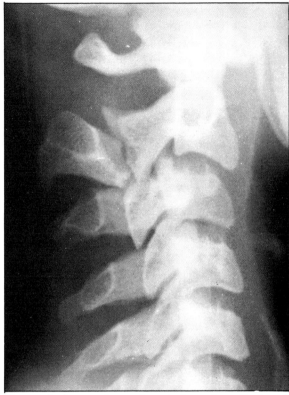

X-ray of a fractured second cervical vertebrae. Such neck fractures should always be treated as serious injuries.

Neck injuries

The sports where neck fractures can occur are rugby, surfing, water-skiing and diving (especially into shallow water or surf with underlying sand-bars). Any significant injury to the head or neck which causes neck or arm pain should be treated with respect. If the pain is severe and present on even slight neck movements, or if there is pain, numbness or weakness in the arms, trunk or legs, then the player needs medical attention immediately.

Caution: The injured person should only be handled by experts and, until help arrives, the neck can be carefully immobilized by placing rolled up towels or blankets on either side of the head and neck. Under no circumstances must the casualty be moved in such a way as to cause bending or any movement of the head relative to the body before or during transport to hospital.

Minor neck strain (*'wry neck'*)

This is a common condition and can occur in any sport. Pain can come on suddenly after a particular movement, or gradually. Pain is worse on neck movement and the head may be tilted to one side by the muscle spasm.

Treatment
Local heat, pain-killing tablets and occasionally muscle relaxants. A neck collar and traction may be provided by a physiotherapist. Symptoms should improve within 5-7 days.

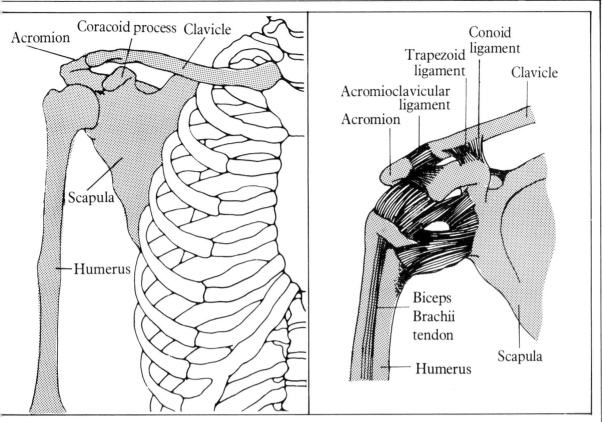

Shoulder injuries

Acromio-clavicular joint injury

This is a small joint at the outer end of the collarbone (or clavicle) where it is attached to the shoulder blade. It is commonly injured in a fall either onto the point of the shoulder or the elbow. This injury is often seen in sports such as rugby and wrestling where direct blows are frequent. It can also occur in cycling, riding, skiing and gymnastics where a person may fall heavily. Usually this injury is a ligament sprain at the joint but occasionally these ligaments may rupture. In this instance, a 'lump' or 'step' becomes visible at the outer end of the collarbone.

Treatment
Minor sprains respond to rest until the pain has settled. Mobility exercises are important early on. In more serious injuries or dislocations, an X-ray may be needed and a longer period of rest and rehabilitation organised. If pain is severe or continues, a doctor should be consulted. Strapping will be of little

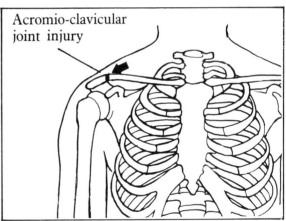

Shoulder joint injuries are frequent in rugby and wrestling where direct blows or falls are common.

benefit. This injury should be treated more seriously in sportsmen where stability of this joint is important (i.e., in weight-lifters or prop forwards in rugby) so that they can return to their activities as soon as possible.

Fractures of the collarbone *(clavicle)*

This bone is frequently broken in falls onto

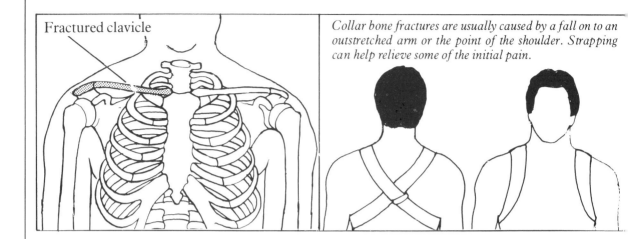

Fractured clavicle

Collar bone fractures are usually caused by a fall on to an outstretched arm or the point of the shoulder. Strapping can help relieve some of the initial pain.

the shoulder or outstretched arm. It is common in contact sports but can also occur in skiing, cycling and riding. There is pain, tenderness and swelling along the bone itself and there may be a visible deformity.

Treatment

A doctor must be consulted and an X-ray taken. A figure-of-eight strapping may be of benefit to ease the pain initially but is not essential and may not be prescribed. These fractures usually heal in about 4-8 weeks during which contact sports should be avoided.

Dislocation of the shoulder

This is a common injury in sportsmen and sportswomen. Notable cases are Bryan Robson, the England footballer who has had recurrent problems and Terry Alderman, the Australian test cricketer who dislocated his shoulder in a fall while trying to apprehend a spectator. It may occur in almost any sport where a person falls onto an outstretched arm with the shoulder in its least stable position – i.e., with the arm lifted upwards and sideways and the player landing on that arm forcing it backwards. Pain is immediate, coupled with an inability to move the arm and there may also be an obvious distortion of the normal shoulder shape. Occasionally, the shoulder is dislocated when the arm is pulled forcibly outwards and backwards by an opponent – for example, in rugby, wrestling or American football. Recurrent dislocation may follow on from this initial injury and can occur with simple falls or even during a normal movement such as raising the arm behind the head.

Treatment

The injured player must see a doctor as soon as possible after the injury. The earlier the shoulder is manipulated back into position the easier this is and the quicker the healing period. An X-ray is needed to check the position of the shoulder and to check for a fracture. A sling is worn for at least three weeks or the arm is strapped against the body (wearing a jumper over the arm is useful) to support the shoulder and allow healing of the injured joint capsule and ligaments. Gentle mobility exercises are begun at two to four weeks.

In recurrent dislocation, the shoulder becomes increasingly easy to reposition and the individual or another person may manage to do this by firmly (but not jerkily) pulling on the arm while stabilizing the trunk and shoulder socket. When dislocation has occurred more than three or four times, surgery may be necessary to stabilize the joint and an adequate period of rehabilitation is essential before a return to sporting activity.

Unstable shoulder joint (*subluxation of the shoulder*)

A person may feel as if his or her shoulder 'has slipped out of joint and gone back in'. This feeling of instability is due to a sliding movement of the shoulder joint but is not a proper dislocation. It is most noticeable when the arm is lifted up to the side and the hand rotated backwards as in a throwing movement. Polevaulters, baseball pitchers, basketball players and racquet players may complain of this.

Treatment
If symptoms continue despite a programme of exercises to strengthen the shoulder muscles, a doctor should be consulted.

Sternoclavicular joint injury

This small joint at the inner end of the collarbone where it joins the breastbone (sternum)

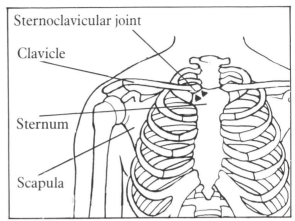

Injuries to the sternoclavicular joint are generally the result of a direct blow or fall.

is supported by ligaments which may be injured in a heavy fall or impact, as can happen in rugby or American football. Tenderness and swelling is felt over the joint.

Treatment
Ice and rest, followed by a gradual return to activity is usually adequate. If pain persists, see a doctor.

Tendon injuries of the shoulder

The shoulder joint is supported by a group of small muscles and tendons called the rotator cuff. These four short tendons hold the upper end of the arm bone (humerus) in the shoulder socket. Sudden forceful injuries (as occur in wrestling, rugby, team handball, American football) may lead to a small tear or rarely (usually in older people) a complete rupture of one of these tendons. Excessive repetitive movements of the shoulder, as in throwing or racquet sports, swimming or weight-lifting, can cause swelling and inflammation of one of these tendons (tendinitis). This swollen tendon then gets 'pinched' between the shoulder and arm bones during certain movements. This is usually on raising the arm out to the side (abduction) and this is called the 'painful arc' sign.

In an acute injury where there is a tear to one of these tendons (caused by falling onto the point of the shoulder or the outstretched arm, wrenching of the arm by an opponent, lifting or throwing heavy objects) pain is immediately felt in the shoulder but occasionally felt in the upper arm. There is

The head (upper end) of the right humerus has moved downwards and forwards relative to the shoulder joint cavity.

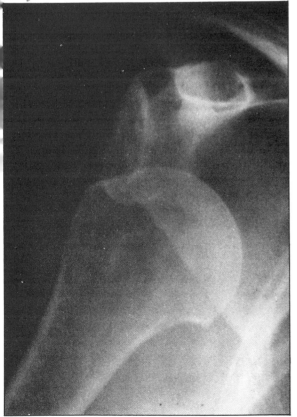

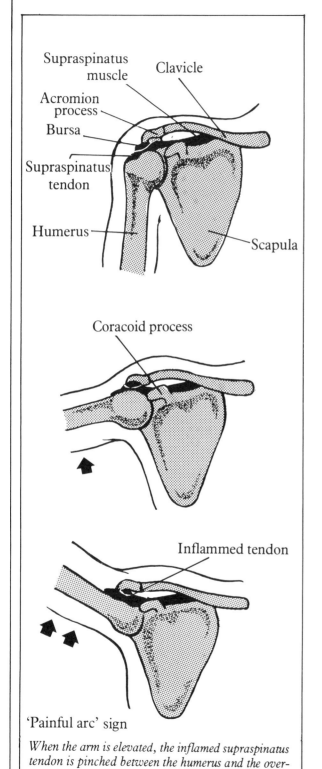

Supraspinatus muscle
Clavicle
Acromion process
Bursa
Supraspinatus tendon
Humerus
Scapula

Coracoid process

Inflammed tendon

'Painful arc' sign

When the arm is elevated, the inflamed supraspinatus tendon is pinched between the humerus and the overhanging acromion process. This pressure is relieved as the arm is elevated fully.

difficulty in moving the arm and it may feel weak. In the case of overuse leading to an inflamed tendon, pain is less acute and gradually increases over days or even weeks. It is felt on certain movements of the arm and there may be tenderness over the tip or front of the shoulder. The 'painful arc' sign is helpful in the diagnosis. The pain will be reproduced by moving the arm against resistance, thereby stressing the affected tendon even more.

Treatment
Acute tear: Ice followed by rest for 48 hours, then gentle mobility exercises. See a doctor if symptoms do not settle early, if there is persistent weakness or an inability to move the arm.

Overuse injury: This will only respond to adequate rest and avoidance of aggravating activities. Gentle pendulum exercises are important to maintain mobility. Physiotherapy is helpful. If pain persists, see a doctor who may recommend a steroid (cortisone) injection, after which rest is absolutely essential for a week or so. Return to sport depends on the severity of the tendinitis. The earlier that rest is started, the sooner the sport can be resumed. This should be when the pain has settled (often 1-3 weeks or even longer). A too rapid return to sport may lead to a chronic problem which is much more difficult to treat. Calcium deposits may form in the tendon itself in chronic cases and older patients. These deposits can go on to cause further problems.

Biceps tendinitis

The biceps muscle in the upper arm is responsible for bending (flexing) the elbow. It has a long tendon which crosses the front of the shoulder joint and which may become inflamed and painful with vigorous throwing movements, canoeing, swimming or weightlifting. Pain is felt at the front of the shoulder during movements such as reaching behind one's back to put on a coat sleeve or do up a

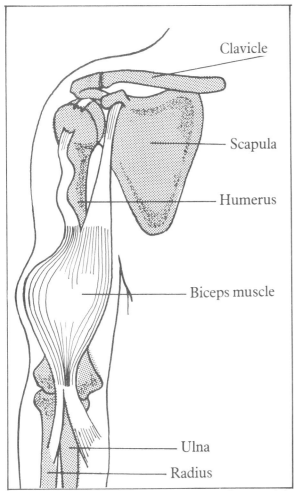

Vigorous throwing movements used in canoeing or weight lifting can cause inflammation of the biceps muscle and sometimes even rupture as shown here.

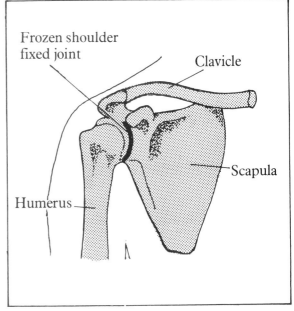

Frozen shoulder is characterised by a painful, stiff shoulder and often occurs in middle-aged sportsmen after a minor injury or for no apparent reason.

bra strap. There may be tenderness over the front of the shoulder and pain is felt on arm elevation and elbow bending against resistance. Occasionally this tendon can rupture, in which case there is a history of a sudden injury, immediate pain, swelling and marked weakness when attempting to bend the elbow. A doctor should be consulted in this instance.

Treatment
Rest and physiotherapy.

Frozen shoulder (*Adhesive capsulitis*)

This condition usually occurs in people aged 40-60 years old and may follow a seemingly trivial injury or occur without warning. The lining of the shoulder joint itself (capsule) becomes inflamed and contracts to give rise to a painful stiff shoulder. At first, pain is slight but it increases gradually and is often severe at night. Pain occurs at rest as well as with shoulder movement and is slowly replaced by stiffness over weeks or months. This stiffness can last for 6-18 months.

Treatment
Pain-killing tablets (such as aspirin or paracetamol) and injections can help in the initial period while vigorous physiotherapy is important later on to keep the shoulder as mobile as possible.

Fibrositis

This is a common term used to describe a poorly-understood localized condition where there are one or more painful spots in certain muscles. The shoulders are frequently affected. Tender hard areas or 'knots' may be felt in the muscle. There is no evidence of inflammation or injury in this condition.

Treatment
Heat and massage. The condition does not usually preclude sporting activity.

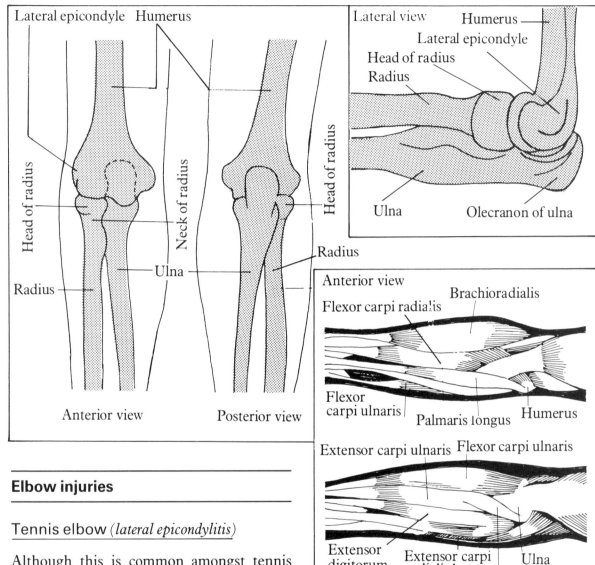

Lateral epicondyle   Humerus

Head of radius

Radius

Neck of radius

Ulna

Radius

Anterior view

Head of radius

Posterior view

Lateral view   Humerus

Lateral epicondyle

Head of radius

Radius

Ulna

Olecranon of ulna

Anterior view

Flexor carpi radialis

Brachioradialis

Flexor carpi ulnaris

Palmaris longus

Humerus

Extensor carpi ulnaris

Flexor carpi ulnaris

Extensor digitorum

Extensor carpi radialis longus

Ulna

Anconeus

Posterior view

Elbow injuries

Tennis elbow (*lateral epicondylitis*)

Although this is common amongst tennis players, it is seen in golfers and many other racquet sports. It is also very common in certain manual occupations and other leisure activities. This is an overuse injury at the site where the muscles in the forearm which extend (or cock-up) the wrist are attached at the elbow. Pain and tenderness is felt over the outside (lateral) point of the elbow near a small bony protruberance which can be felt there. Excessive and repetitive movements at the wrist (gripping, twisting and untwisting) or backhand shots in tennis, squash and badminton cause stretching and strain of this tendon and straightening or extending the

wrist against resistance will bring on the pain at the elbow.

In racquet sports (particularly tennis), a faulty backhand technique may bring on and aggravate this problem. In tennis, this occurs when a player predominantly uses a wrist action, rather than using a firm wrist and the whole trunk, arm and shoulder, to hit the ball. If the racquet is too heavy or the grip too big or small, then this may also lead to problems. Heavy balls, fast court surfaces

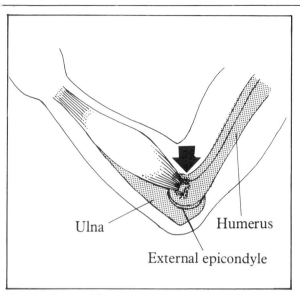

Ulna

Humerus

External epicondyle

Tennis elbow afflicts many manual workers, gardeners and home handymen, as well as sportsmen.

such as grass and a tightly-strung racquet are all factors that increase the load of impact on the wrist.

Treatment

Ice initially followed by heat and physiotherapy (ultrasound) after 48 hours. Movements which aggravate the pain should be avoided. Local steroid injections by the doctor are effective in the more severe cases. It is important to rest early and allow adequate tissue healing to take place (days in mild cases to weeks in more severe ones). Once pain has settled, strengthening exercises to the wrist extensor muscles can be started. Faulty playing equipment and technique should be corrected. A firm circular strap (2.5 cm / 1 inch in diameter) wrapped around the upper part of the forearm 5-7.5 cm (2-3 inches below the elbow, may help in chronic cases as a preventative measure.

Golfer's elbow / 'thrower's' elbow (*medial epicondylitis*)

Similar to tennis elbow, this condition arises where there is excessive strain or stretching of the flexor muscles of the forearm where they attach to the inner (or medial) side of the elbow. These muscles bend the wrist palm downwards and provide finger grip. Rapid,

forceful bending of the wrist with a closed grip (and turning the forearm inwards at the same time) can bring this on. This movement occurs in javelin-throwers, golfers (with a faulty bottom-handed technique particularly), baseball pitchers, cricket bowlers, and in tennis players with a fast service or exaggerated topspin.

Treatment

As for tennis elbow.

Little-league elbow

This is a throwing injury that occurs in growing individuals and is seen in young baseball pitchers. In children and adolescents, the muscles attached on the inner side of the elbow are fixed on to a growing piece of bone (the epiphysis) which can separate

Golfer's elbow is not confined to golfers – it is also a common injury among javelin-throwers.

from the main bone with continued traction and strain.

Treatment
Adequate rest and rehabilitation for eight weeks at least. Surgery may be necessary if separation is significant.

Ulnar neuritis

The ulnar nerve runs under the inner side of the elbow and if struck by a blow, there is an intense, painful, tingling sensation – hence the term 'funny-bone'. In some cases, the nerve may be irritated by the repetitive movements of throwing or racquet sports. Pain is usually accompanied by numbness which affects the ring and little finger of that hand. The nerve can be felt at the inside of the elbow and is often tender.

Treatment
Rest. In persistent cases, surgery may be necessary to free the nerve in order to protect it from further injury.

Triceps strain

Pain at the back of the elbow may occur when there is a strain or occasionally a

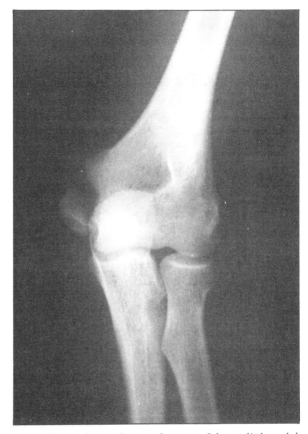

This X-ray picture shows a fracture of the medial condyle of the humerus bone.

rupture of the triceps tendon, which is responsible for straightening the elbow. Tenderness is felt at the back of and just above the point of the elbow. Straightening the elbow against resistance is painful. Javelin and ball throwers may be affected or symptoms can follow a fall onto the arm.

Treatment
Rest and ice. If weakness is severe, see a doctor. Once pain has settled, strengthening exercise can be gradually commenced.

Student's elbow *(Olecranon bursitis)*

Just over the tip of the elbow is a small sack of fluid (bursa) which protects the point of the bone (*olecranon*). A direct blow here, or repeated pressure can cause swelling and

Student's elbow is caused by repeated pressure on the tip of the elbow or by a direct blow to it.

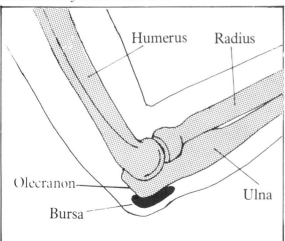

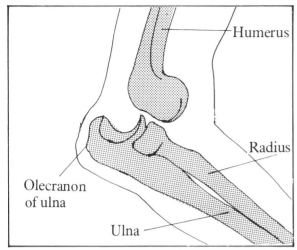

Elbow dislocation is usually caused by a fall on the hand when the elbow is bent.

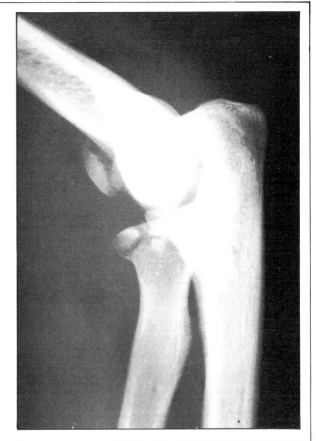

inflammation of the bursa (bursitis). This results in pain and tenderness and an obvious swelling at the point of the elbow. Elbow guards act as protection to prevent this sort of injury in ice hockey, roller-skating, skateboarding and American football.

Treatment
Rest and firm strapping. See a doctor if swelling is marked or symptoms continue.

Elbow dislocation

This is a severe injury that can occur in contact sports where, for example, the player falls onto the hand with the elbow bent. There is pain, swelling and obvious deformity of the elbow. Soft-tissue damage to ligaments is severe and rehabilitation is lengthy.

Treatment
Medical attention must be sought immediately.

Fractures of the head of the forearm bone *(radius)*

A heavy fall onto the outstretched arm can cause a small, crush fracture of the top of one of the forearm bones (radius). The symptoms may not be severe and therefore this fracture can often go undetected. Pain is felt at the outer aspect of the elbow, particularly

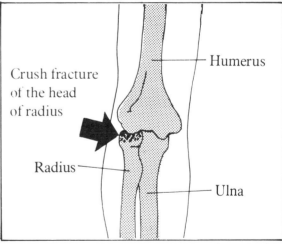

Because symptoms are not very obvious, a fracture of the head of the forearm bone can often go unnoticed.

with twisting of the forearm or full straightening of the elbow.

Treatment
If in doubt, consult a doctor who will arrange an X-ray. Rehabilitation, once commenced, should be aimed at restoring full movement to the elbow.

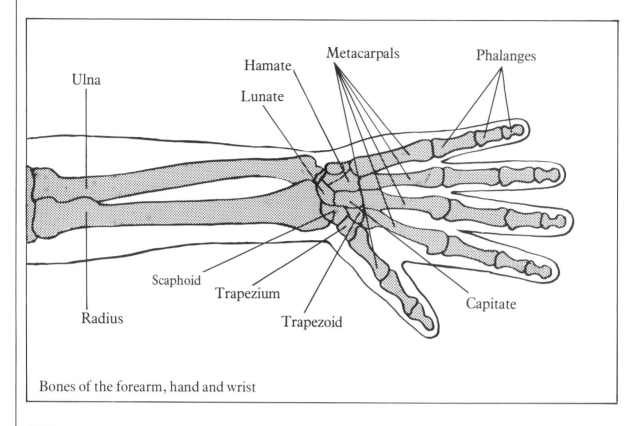

Bones of the forearm, hand and wrist

Forearm and wrist injuries

De Quervain's tenosynovitis

Excessive repetitive movement of the wrist can cause inflammation of the long tendons of the forearm and wrist. The commonest injury involves those tendons which perform thumb movements and which lie on the thumb side of the wrist (de Quervain's tenosynovitis). Oarsmen are frequently affected, especially if they have an exaggerated 'feathering' technique. Racquet players are also at risk. There is pain, swelling, tenderness and often 'creaking' (crepitus) over the affected tendons. Stretching the tendon causes pain.

Treatment
Rest is essential until all signs of inflammation have settled. Anti-inflammatory medication, physiotherapy and/or steroid injections can be used to speed up healing.

Chronic cases or oarsmen who are prevented from continuing active competition may benefit from surgery to free the inflamed tendon from its surrounding sheath.

Fractures of the scaphoid

The scaphoid is a small bone in the wrist located at the base of the thumb where it joins onto the wrist joint. This bone has a very fragile blood supply and therefore fractures may heal poorly. It can fracture in falls onto an extended arm, with the wrist and hand being forcibly bent backwards. This may occur in any sport but is more likely in contact sports. Symptoms are pain and tenderness with occasional swelling in the hollow at the base of the thumb (most noticeable with the thumb bent back towards the wrist), and there is usually reduced grip power.

Treatment
This injury may resemble a simple wrist

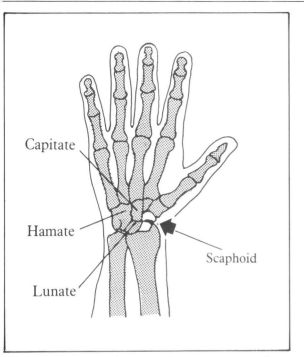

Scaphoid fractures often occur in contact sports after a fall, when the wrist and hand are bent backwards.

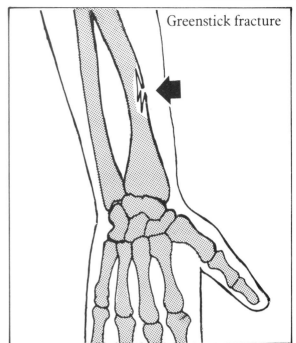

Greenstick fractures usually affect children and are often the result of a fall.

sprain. If there is any doubt, any localized tenderness or if symptoms persist for several days, then a doctor should be seen. A plaster cast is usually worn for 6-12 weeks but a close check is needed to ensure adequate bone healing.

Greenstick fractures

The forearm bones of children are less brittle than in adults and can bend slightly. This can result in a 'rippling' type of fracture on one side of the bone. These are called greenstick fractures and there may only be moderate pain and swelling. Localized bony tenderness of the lower end of the forearm after a fall is a clue to such an injury.

Treatment
If in doubt, see a doctor.

Wrist sprains

The wrist is a very mobile joint (particularly so in some young women with supple joints) and is commonly injured in falls. Mostly these involve minor sprains of the wrist

ligaments which respond well to ice, rest and simple strapping.

Treatment
When the pain has settled, strengthening exercises can be started. If pain is severe, if there is any visible deformity of the wrist, if a grating sensation is felt or if there is an obvious loss of movement, an X-ray is needed to check for a possible fracture.

Hand injuries

Fractures of hand or fingers

Fractures of the hand or fingers are common in contact sports such as boxing, rugby and American football, or in ball games such as cricket, basketball, volleyball and handball. The injury may be caused by a fall or a direct blow, either from an opponent (for example, stamping in rugby) or the ball (for example, fielding in cricket). Symptoms are pain, swelling and tenderness. There may be an

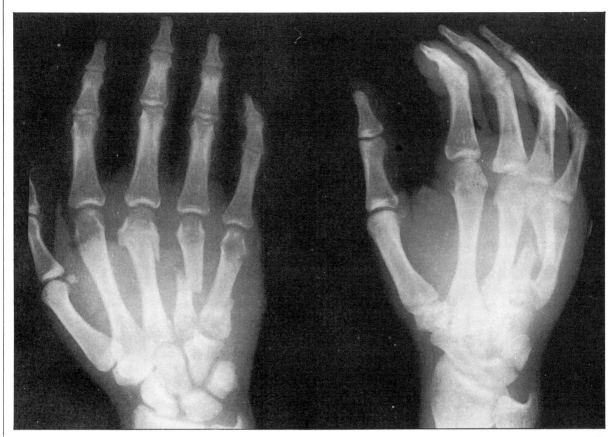

X-rayed fracture of the metacarpals, a common injury in contact sports and ball games when it is either the result of a fall or a direct blow.

obvious deformity and grating may be felt at the site of the injury.

Treatment

If the bones are not greatly displaced, treatment is straightforward. For hand fractures, a simple bandage or occasionally a light plaster cast for 3-4 weeks is sufficient. In finger fractures, it is essential to keep the fingers mobile (unless the fracture is unstable). Strapping two fingers together is all that is needed for the first few days. After that, movement should be encouraged. Contact sports should be avoided till the fracture has healed.

Thumb sprains

This happens when the thumb is forced backwards, as in a rugby tackle or catching a basketball awkwardly. In minor sprains, there is pain and tenderness but minimal swelling and relatively full movement. A more severe sprain, or rupture, of the thumb ligaments is an extremely common Alpine skiing injury. Here, the thumb is forced upwards and backwards by the skier's pole handle during a fall, thereby rupturing the ligaments at the inside of the base of the thumb. Pain is severe and there is tenderness in the thumb web with associated bruising and swelling. The thumb may feel unstable.

Treatment

For minor sprains, firm-support strapping after ice and rest should allow an early return to sport. For a severe sprain or rupture, rest, ice, compression and elevation should be followed by an early medical opinion. A plaster cast, or in some cases surgery, may be necessary.

Finger sprains

The small joints of the fingers are supported by ligaments that are easily sprained in sports such as rugby, basketball, volleyball, handball and cricket. There is pain, swelling and tenderness over the affected joint and the finger develops increasing stiffness. The stiffness and swelling can persist for many weeks, often for up to 6-12 months. It is important to keep the finger moving to prevent chronic immobility.

Treatment
Strapping is only necessary for comfort and should not be encouraged for mild sprains. Early mobility exercises are important.

Dislocation of the fingers

This can occur in the same situations as for finger sprains. The pain is more severe and there is loss of movement and deformity of the finger.

Treatment
Rapid manipulation of the joint to its original position is important. If done quickly, then the healing period is shorter and this procedure is less painful. Taping the finger to the adjacent digit for a week, or days even, is usually sufficient. Early mobility exercises are important. Early return to sport is possible, providing the finger is protected by strapping. An X-ray should be taken to check for a small fracture.

Mallet finger *(extensor tendon rupture)*

Here there has been a complete rupture of the tendon which is responsible for straightening the end joint of the finger. A direct blow on the fingertip which forces this last joint to bend abruptly is usually responsible. Goalkeeping in soccer, catching a baseball or cricket ball can cause this. The tell-tale sign is an inability to straighten (extend) this last joint, with the fingertip being characteristically bent at an angle. There is tenderness below the nail just above this joint.

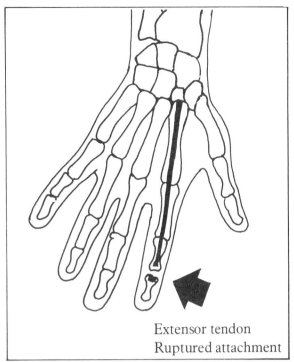

Extensor tendon
Ruptured attachment

Mallet finger, usually caused by a direct blow to the fingertips, is a common injury in goalkeepers and also fielders in baseball and cricket.

Treatment
The finger should be immobilised in a finger splint for a period of 3-4 weeks.

Blacknail *(subungual haematoma)*

Direct blows to the nail can cause bleeding under the nail itself. Pain can be quite severe.

Treatment
An effective and rapid treatment is to sterilize a pin or paperclip with a flame and then to press this down onto the nail (this is a painless procedure as there are no nerves in the nail) in order to make a small hole. The blood clot can then escape and pain relief is instantaneous.

Finger infections

Any infection of the finger or hand must be taken seriously. If in any doubt, see a doctor.

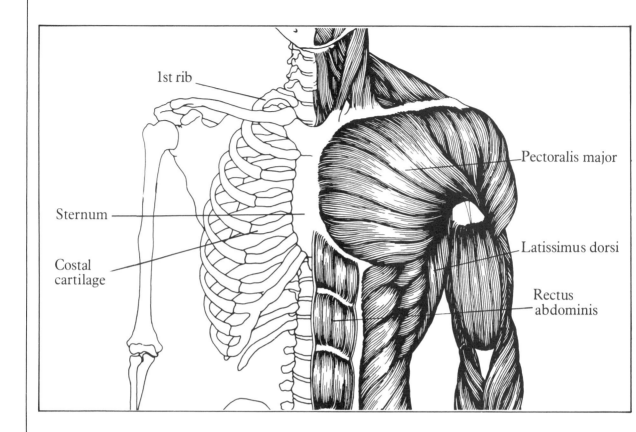

1st rib

Sternum

Costal cartilage

Pectoralis major

Latissimus dorsi

Rectus abdominis

Chest injuries

Rib injuries

Direct blows to the chest are common in contact sports. Bruising to the ribs often results in pain, tenderness and occasional swelling. More severe localized tenderness with pain felt on taking in a deep breath is suggestive of a rib fracture. In this case 'grating' can sometimes be felt at the point of tenderness. Severe rib fractures can damage the underlying lung and chest cavity. Breathlessness (especially if it is increasing) requires immediate medical attention.

Treatment
Ice and rest for simple bruising. If a fracture is suspected, it is important to have an X-ray before resuming any form of contact sport. Strapping is of no real benefit in the treatment of fractured ribs.

Rib cartilage injuries

Sideways compression of the rib-cage (for example, during a collapsed scrum or ruck in rugby) can cause a sprain or even dislocation of the rib cartilages near their attachment to the breastbone (sternum). Pain, swelling and localized tenderness to one side of the breastbone, often with a visible lump, are the signs to look for.

Treatment
Rest and ice. Physiotherapy may help.

Stitch

Most people experience this at some time in their sporting life. It is characterised by a sharp pain felt under the rib-cage (usually to one side) and commonly comes on during exercise soon after a meal (especially if fizzy drinks have been taken). Pain is cramp-like

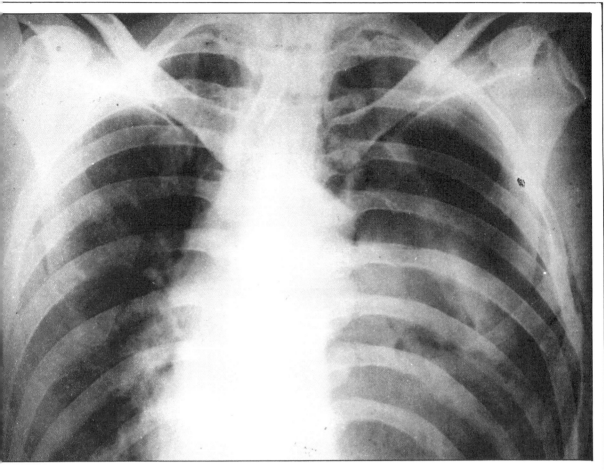

X-ray of fractured ribs, a fairly common injury in contact sports and the result of a direct blow to the chest. In severe cases, lung damage can occur.

Fractured rib
and damaged
rib cartilage

and is directly related to effort. It is made worse on breathing out and relieved by a deep breath in.

Treatment
In the acute situation, the stitch can be relieved by bending forward while running, by breath-holding or by squeezing a small object firmly (according to some sources). The best treatment is prevention – by not exercising too soon after meals and by means of adequate warm up. The exact cause of stitch is not known but it may be related to spasm and/or a reduction in blood supply to the muscle of the diaphragm.

The symptoms of rib cartilage injuries are pain, swelling and tenderness to one side of the breast bone.

Backache and back injuries

Although back problems frequently affect active sportsmen and women, there are few injuries that are directly attributable to their sport. In many cases, there are underlying minor spinal disorders that only become a problem as the individual becomes more active and puts a strain on the spine. Poor posture is also a major factor in backache and much has been written on this subject. Rather than discuss individual conditions, here are some simple guidelines to help in the diagnosis and general care of back pain.

Causes of back pain

The majority of cases of back pain in the athlete are due to **muscle strain** which typically comes on during or after sport. Pain is felt in the back, often to one side, and there is stiffness and some loss of mobility. If pain comes on acutely and is felt in the buttock and/or the leg, or if there is any numbness, pins and needles, or weakness in the leg, then a **slipped disc** (disc prolapse) should be suspected. This means that the disc which acts as a cushion between two vertebrae has 'burst' and is pressing on a nerve to the leg. This pain is called **sciatica**. Pain due to a muscle strain will usually settle within a few days, but sciatica and pain from a slipped disc (which can occur without sciatica) usually lasts for much longer. Direct blows onto the spine can cause **vertebral fractures**, as can falls from a height (for example, in horse-riding) or situations where a player is forcibly and sharply bent over forwards.

Treatment
In the case of a simple muscle strain, rest, local heat and then mobility and strengthening exercises are usually adequate. Abdominal muscles are important in the support of the spine and care should be taken to strengthen them. Bilateral straight-leg raises (raising both legs straight off the ground while lying on one's back) are ex-

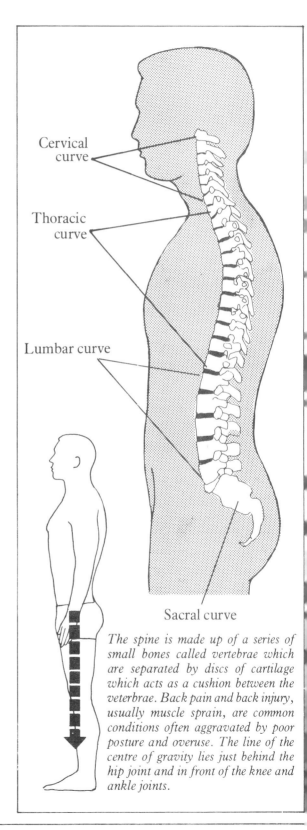

Cervical curve

Thoracic curve

Lumbar curve

Sacral curve

The spine is made up of a series of small bones called vertebrae which are separated by discs of cartilage which acts as a cushion between the veterbrae. Back pain and back injury, usually muscle sprain, are common conditions often aggravated by poor posture and overuse. The line of the centre of gravity lies just behind the hip joint and in front of the knee and ankle joints.

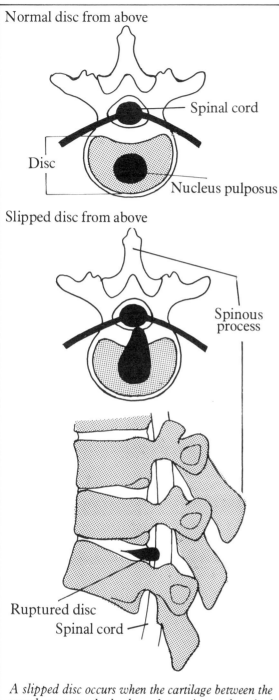

Normal disc from above

Spinal cord

Disc

Nucleus pulposus

Slipped disc from above

Spinous process

Ruptured disc

Spinal cord

A slipped disc occurs when the cartilage between the vertebrae protrudes backwards pressing on the spinal cord, causing severe pain.

tremely bad exercises for anyone with a history of back trouble and should be avoided. Abdominal exercises should always be performed with the knees and hips bent up and the feet on the ground (then raising the shoulders off the ground).

In general terms, advice should be sought regarding posture, bedding and chair supports to correct any underlying factors that may contribute to a back problem. Care with lifting is essential. Before returning to sport, symptoms should have settled, a strengthening programme should be under way and adequate stretching and warm up should be carried out before exercise.

Back pain requiring medical attention

● Severe back pain ●·Sciatica ● Back pain aggravated by coughing or sneezing ● Back pain which has not settled within 48-72 hours ● Back pain with no history of injury as a cause ● Back pain where there is localized tenderness over the spine itself.

Injuries to the genitalia

Direct blows to the testicles are extremely painful and may even cause fainting. Bruising can be quite marked and should be treated initially with cold packs. Protective devices are essential in certain sports to avoid injury. It should be noted that sterility can result from repeated or severe injury to the testes.

Torsion or twisting of the testicle is a condition which causes severe pain and is occasionally seen in cyclists. It requires immediate medical attention. Cyclists are also prone to a rare condition called priapism where there is persistent penile erection due to blockage in the blood supply. Again, this needs urgent medical treatment.

The female genitalia may also bruise after a direct blow, such as falling astride a beam in the gymnasium. In severe cases, a fracture of a small bone in the pelvis (pubis) can result. Female water-skiers must wear rubber wetsuit pants at all times (even in the hot climates of Australia and the Mediterranean). A high-speed fall on the water can result in a forced douching which can cause lacerations or, more importantly, severe internal injury (especially in the case of salt water).

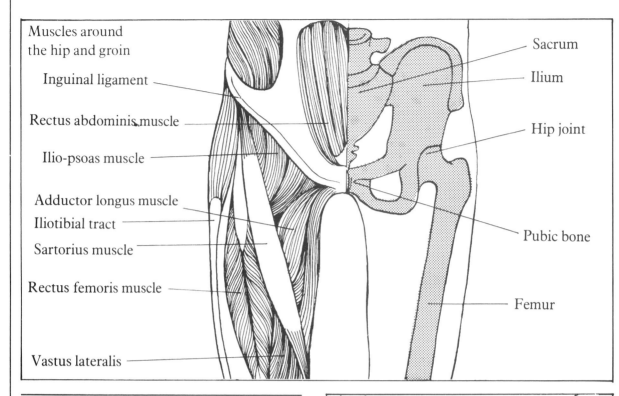

Muscles around
the hip and groin

Inguinal ligament

Rectus abdominis muscle

Ilio-psoas muscle

Adductor longus muscle

Iliotibial tract

Sartorius muscle

Rectus femoris muscle

Vastus lateralis

Sacrum

Ilium

Hip joint

Pubic bone

Femur

Hip and groin injuries

There are many causes of pain in this region
but there are clues to look for in deciding on a
diagnosis. Sharp pain felt in the groin, which
comes on during a sudden movement, is
likely to be a muscle or tendon strain. These
usually settle with rest and local heat, followed by gentle stretching and mobility
exercises once the pain has settled. Early rest
is important.

More gradual or chronic pain in the groin
can be due to a variety of causes which may
or may not be related to exercise. Examples
are hernia, inflammation of lymph glands, a
'trapped' nerve in the spine, or, in the older
patient especially, arthritis of the hip joint. If
pain persists despite rest, then see a doctor.

Groin strain *(adductor strain)*

This is a strain of the muscles on the inside of
the thigh high up in the groin region. Footballers are frequently affected but it is also

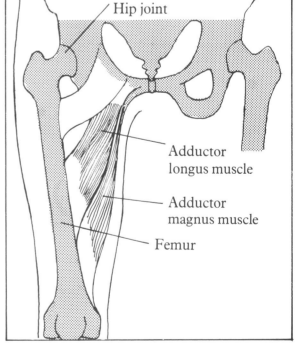

Hip joint

Adductor
longus muscle

Adductor
magnus muscle

Femur

*Groin strain is characterised by pain on the inner upper
side of the thigh when the adductor muscles are stretched.
This is common in footballers.*

common amongst horse-riders, hurdlers, sprinters, jumpers, ice-skaters and ice-hockey players. The pain can come on suddenly (often early on in the training when warm up has been inadequate) or gradually when there has been a period of intensive training or activity. Tenderness is felt over the prominent tendon high up inside the thigh. Pain is brought on by pressing the legs together against resistance.

Treatment
Rest and heat followed by physiotherapy in more severe or chronic cases. Gradual return to sport is advised with an emphasis on gentle stretching, flexibility exercises and, later, strengthening exercises. In acute injuries, ice packs may help to control the bruising and swelling.

Hip flexor strain (*ilio-psoas strain*)

This muscle is responsible for bending the hip, i.e. bringing the thigh forward as in kicking or climbing. It is a deep muscle and pain is felt deep in the groin over the front of the hip joint. Pain is produced when bending the hip against resistance. The many causes of hip flexor strain include hurdling, steeple-chasing, high- and long-jumping, fell-running and mountaineering, running in heavy or snowy conditions, cross-country, skiing, rowing, football (especially shooting practice) and weight-training.

Other muscles affected in this region include the rectus femoris (part of the quadriceps) and the abdominal muscles. Treatment principles are the same.

Treatment
As for groin strain.

Stress fractures of the hip (*femur*)

These can occur in long-distance road runners as a result of the repeated load on the leg. If pain persists in the hip region and comes on with running or jumping or if there is a chronic ache after activity, with pain on hip movement, then see your doctor as an X-ray may be advisable. A repeat X-ray 3-4 weeks later may be necessary if symptoms continue, as these fractures do not show up early on X-rays. Treatment depends on the

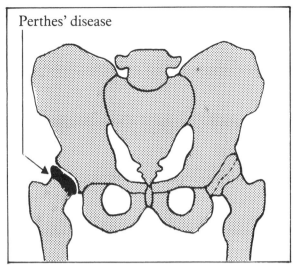

In Perthes' disease, the upper part of the femur degenerates as it enters the hip joint.

level of pain but rest from sport is necessary until the bone has healed.

Osteitis pubis

Chronic pain in the pubic region over the bony joint directly above and behind the genitalia (this joint is the pubic symphysis), where the two sides of the pelvis meet, is common in soccer-players and in other sports where there is repeated kicking, side-stepping and tackling. This is an overuse injury.

Treatment
An X-ray is often useful to confirm this condition. Rest is important. If the pain does not settle, then the doctor may recommend anti-inflammatory tablets, physiotherapy, or occasionally steroid injections.

Hip problems in children and adolescents

There are several causes of hip pain in this age group which require early diagnosis. The growing part of the thigh bone where it enters the hip joint may slip (slipped epiphysis) and cause groin and/or knee pain. Boys aged 10-15 years are most at risk and sporting activity can bring this on. Children aged 4-10 years can develop a degenerative condition of the hip (Perthe's disease) which results in pain and a limp. Any child or adolescent with a limp due to hip or knee pain (or even a painless limp) must see a doctor. An X-ray will confirm the diagnosis.

Iliac crest epiphysitis

The upper rim of the pelvis, at the level of the waistline, is the site of a growing area of bone (epiphysis) in the adolescent. Pain on one side can occur when repeated exercise or violent twisting involving the abdominal muscles causes inflammation or separation of this bony growth area.

Treatment
Rest and physiotherapy. Once growth has ceased and the bones have joined completely, there is no risk of this recurring.

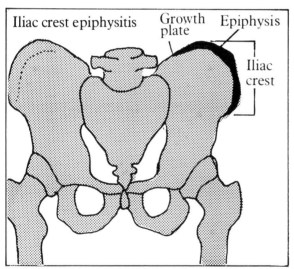

The iliac crest epiphysis can be the site of pain and inflammation in adolescent athletes.

Runner's hip (*Trochanteric bursitis*)

Pain and tenderness on the outer aspect of the upper thigh is a common problem in runners. This is usually an overuse injury and is felt after a long run (road-running particularly) or hard training. There is tenderness over the bony point at the outside of the hip where a small sac of fluid (or bursa) sits over the bone separating it from the over-lying muscles. It is this sac that gets inflamed (bursitis). Similar symptoms occur when there is an overuse strain of the muscles in this region (the gluteal muscles).

Treatment
Rest, heat and physiotherapy (particularly ultrasound) followed by reduction in amount of road-running. Steroid injection can help the more chronic cases.

Thigh injuries

Hamstring muscle injury

This can either be an overuse strain, as with runners doing excessive training (particularly hill-climbing or speed work), or an acute muscle tear which causes the athlete to pull up suddenly with a sharp pain at the back of the thigh (this can be high up under the buttock or in the muscle belly itself). Severe muscle tears may result in visible bruising and marked weakness. Sprinters, soccer and rugby players, and hurdlers frequently suffer. If not treated carefully, recurrent problems can develop and many a sportsman is seen wearing a thigh bandage to support his 'gammy' thigh.

Oarsmen in particular are troubled by a strain of the lower end of the hamstring muscles where they attach behind the knee. Pain is produced by resisting knee bending and there is usually local tenderness.

Treatment
For an acute injury, rest, ice, compression and elevation, followed by strapping. A proper course of physiotherapy and a rehabilitation progamme should be organised, appropriate to the severity of the injury. If bruising is present, a doctor should be consulted. For chronic overuse strain, rest, physiotherapy and rehabilitation with an emphasis on stretching, flexibility training and later, strengthening. Stride patterns should be assessed, as overstepping is a common cause of recurrence.

Caution: A hamstring strain can very often become a chronic problem because inadequate time is allowed for healing after the initial injury, and if proper warm up and stretching is not carried out prior to exercise. Stretching after exercise is essential to prevent muscle shortening during the cooldown period.

Corked thigh, charley-horse, dead-leg
(Quadriceps haematoma)

A direct blow to the bulky muscles on the front and outer side of the thigh (quadriceps muscle) can be painful and very disabling. A kick or knee during contact sports is a frequent cause. The resulting bruise on the muscle can cause swelling and marked weakness, with the player often limping for several days.

Treatment
Rest, ice, compression and elevation, followed by physiotherapy. Avoidance of heat or exercise for at least 48 hours is important to prevent further bleeding; this can lead to calcification of the blood clot in the muscle tissue (myositis ossificans). After this initial period, gentle stretching, local heat and ultrasound are recommended and later a return to running and strengthening exercises.

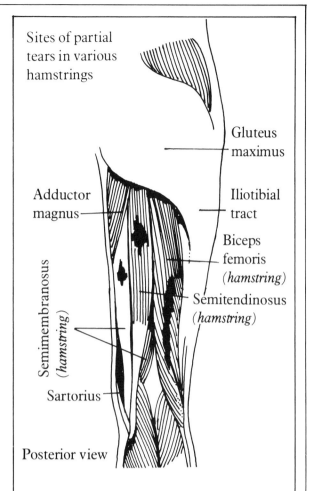

Sites of partial tears in various hamstring muscles. Hamstring strain is particularly common in runners.

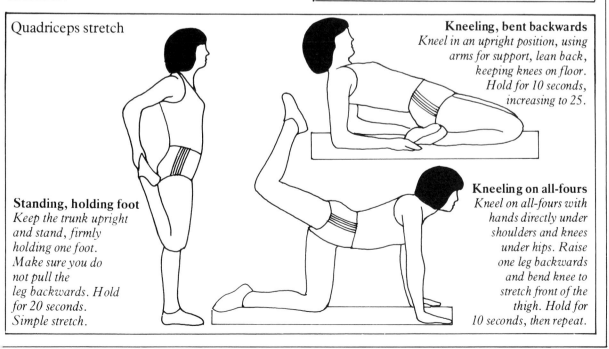

Quadriceps stretch

Kneeling, bent backwards
Kneel in an upright position, using arms for support, lean back, keeping knees on floor. Hold for 10 seconds, increasing to 25.

Standing, holding foot
Keep the trunk upright and stand, firmly holding one foot. Make sure you do not pull the leg backwards. Hold for 20 seconds. Simple stretch.

Kneeling on all-fours
Kneel on all-fours with hands directly under shoulders and knees under hips. Raise one leg backwards and bend knee to stretch front of the thigh. Hold for 10 seconds, then repeat.

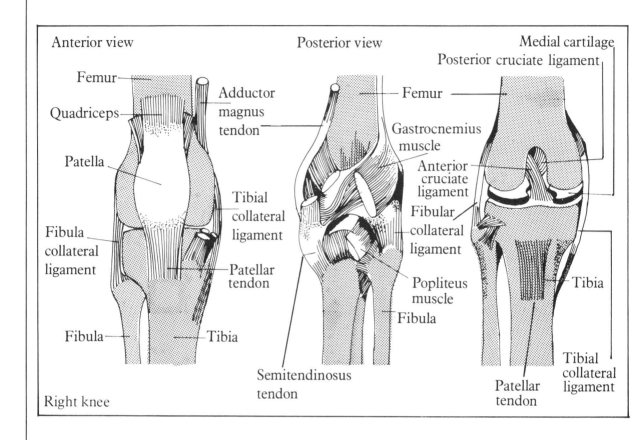

Anterior view — Posterior view — Medial cartilage, Posterior cruciate ligament

Femur — Adductor magnus tendon

Quadriceps — Femur

Patella — Gastrocnemius muscle — Anterior cruciate ligament

Fibula collateral ligament — Tibial collateral ligament — Fibular collateral ligament

Patellar tendon — Popliteus muscle

Fibula — Tibia — Fibula — Tibia

Semitendinosus tendon — Patellar tendon — Tibial collateral ligament

Right knee

Knee injuries

<u>Runner's knee</u> (*Patello-femoral arthralgia, chondromalacia patellae, anterior knee pain*)

Several names have been given to this condition which affects many young athletes. Recent surveys suggest that it is more common amongst adolescent and female athletes. The symptoms are knee pain which is usually felt round or behind the kneecap (patella) but may be poorly localized. The pain tends to be aching and comes on during exercise such as a long run. The increase in pain is often gradual as the person continues to carry out the aggravating activity until eventually even a short jog will bring it on. The pain is typically felt on climbing or descending stairs. Hill-walking and squatting can also aggravate the condition. Some swelling of the knee may occur due to a small build-up of fluid in the joint (effusion). The onset of pain is occasionally acute and may mimic a cartilage or ligament injury. In this instance, the person may describe a sharp pain in the knee with an associated 'giving way' as he or she pivots, or turns sharply on a bent knee. Pain is less severe than in a ligament or cartilage injury and there is no immediate swelling or local tenderness. Firm pressure down on to the kneecap with the leg straightened and relaxed can be painful, and contraction of the thigh muscles (quadriceps) while this pressure is applied to the kneecap causes acute pain. Grating or creaking is also felt behind this bone.

The mechanism responsible for this pain may be a slight change in the alignment of the patella relative to the groove in the femur in which it normally slides. Any weakness of the muscle at the inside of the knee (the vastus medialis part of the quadriceps) will allow the patella to drift laterally. Other factors which may alter this alignment are knock-knees and, more important, hyper-pronation of the foot (*see* Foot injuries pages 78-81). Repeated minor impacts (for example, falls) or deep squats or knee-bends may also contribute to this condition.

Treatment
Acute pain responds to ice-packs, followed by physiotherapy. After this, and in more chronic cases, a strict programme of exercises to strengthen the vastus medialis muscle is necessary. This muscle works mainly with the knee fully straight or only bent up to 15-20 degrees. Therefore straight-leg exercises are necessary. Prevention involves continuing exercises and correction of hyperpronation by means of orthotics and a review of footwear.

Ligament injuries to the knee

The knee is a potentially unstable joint in that the two bones (tibia and femur) that form the joint rely almost totally upon ligaments and muscles to maintain stability. The bones themselves do not interlock to form a stable bony joint.

There are four main ligaments in the knee. The two collateral ligaments (medial and lateral) stabilize the inner and outer aspects of the joint, while the cruciate ligaments (anterior and posterior), which lie deep inside the joint, maintain anterior-posterior stability – i.e. they control the limits of forward and backward movement, while the collateral ligaments control side to side movement. Active stability of the knee (during movement) is provided by contraction of the muscles around the knee. These are mainly the quadriceps and the hamstrings.

Any injury to one of the knee ligaments must be taken seriously and carefully assessed to see that the knee has not become unstable as a result. The particular ligament injured will depend upon the mechanism of injury. This is usually either a direct impact injury or a twisting injury by a person weight-bearing on that leg.

Contact sports such as rugby, soccer, ice hockey and American football often result in direct impact injuries. Twisting injuries can occur in almost any sport where a person

pivots on one leg (for example, squash, football, basketball) and this form of injury is very common in Alpine skiing where inadequate binding release on the skis during a fall is a major cause of knee ligament injuries.

This injury can be classed as a sprain, partial tear, or complete tear (or rupture) where there is marked instability of the knee.

Collateral ligament injury: The medial ligament which lies on the inside of the knee joint is the most frequently injured. A fall, blow or tackle which forces the joint inwards or the foot outwards will stretch and tear this ligament (as with two soccer players side-footing a ball at the same time). A less common injury is that which forces the knee joint outwards or the foot inwards and this sprains or tears the lateral ligament. Twisting injuries in skiing and football frequently cause medial ligament sprains or tears.

Cruciate ligament injury: These ligaments can be torn in a severe injury of the type described above. An impact onto the front of the knee joint which forces it backwards (hyperextension) will often cause a cruciate

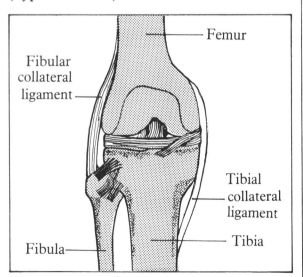

The collateral ligaments in the knee control side to side movements and they are frequently injured in falls, blows and tackles. Note that patella is not shown.

injury as well as damage other tissues around the joint. Tears of the posterior cruciate ligament are less frequent and tend to occur

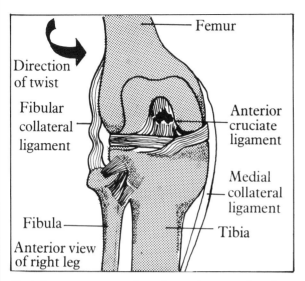

Femur

Direction of twist

Fibular collateral ligament

Anterior cruciate ligament

Medial collateral ligament

Fibula

Tibia

Anterior view of right leg

Twisting movements such as sharp pivots on a bent knee can damage or tear the anterior cruciate ligament.

in severe impact injuries. The anterior cruciate is freqently sprained or torn in twisting injuries and the diagnosis is often confused with a torn cartilage (meniscus). A typical injury occurs when a player pivots sharply on a bent leg with his foot firmly planted on the ground with studs (as in a rapid change of direction at speed).

Symptoms and signs

Pain: This is usually sudden and often severe at the time of the injury but may ease for a while afterwards so that the player can often continue the activity. Severe ligament injuries are too painful for this.

Tenderness: Over the inside or outside of the knee in collateral ligament injuries.

Swelling: Local swelling over collateral ligament tears. In severe injuries or cruciate ligament tears, there will be joint swelling coming on rapidly after the injury. This is due to bleeding into the joint (haemarthrosis).

Instability (giving way): A feeling that the knee is weak, unstable or 'gives way' may come on once the acute injury has settled and the person begins to take weight on the leg

again. This is particularly so in ligament rupture (the commonest being anterior cruciate damage).

Caution: Proper assessment of a significant knee injury should be carried out by a doctor. The presence of swelling inside the joint which has come on rapidly, pain on movement or a loss of movement, severe pain or tenderness, and a feeling of looseness or instability in the joint are all signs that should alert the athlete or sportsman to the need for a medical opinion.

Treatment

For an acute injury, rest, ice, compression and elevation are very important in limiting the swelling. Mild and moderate sprains respond well to physiotherapy and a rehabilitation programme. Severe ligament injuries may require the application of a splint or plaster cast for several weeks. Complete ligament rupture usually requires surgical repair. Pain-killing tablets and anti-inflammatory tablets are useful.

Ligament injuries are often misdiagnosed or ignored initially and repeated injury with inadequate time for healing can give rise to pain, tenderness and instability. Treatment for such chronic injuries is physiotherapy, extensive muscle rehabilitation and occasionally surgery (for chronic instability after anterior cruciate rupture). There are several knee supports and braces available for people with chronic knee instability. These are often bulky but may be the only alternative to surgery where other measures have failed. They are also useful in the postoperative period following a ligament repair, to protect the knee.

Caution: Movement of the knee joint should be full and pain-free before returning to sport. The thigh muscles must be strong and it is essential to do quadriceps muscle exercises early on in the rehabilitation programme even when the leg is immobilised in a plaster cast.

Cartilage injuries (*Meniscus tears*)

The cartilages (menisci) of the knee are like 'spacers' between the two bones of the knee joint and function as shock-absorbers, as well as contributing to the stability and control of movement at that joint. Because of their anatomical position, they can be 'pinched' between the two bones (tibia and femur) in certain movements and a tear can result. The tibia rotates slightly on the femur in full extension of the knee and this increases the likelihood of a cartilage being 'pinched' and torn. These injuries can occur in almost any sport but are most likely in contact sports such as football or rugby.

The medial meniscus at the inner aspect of the knee is torn about four to five times more often than the lateral meniscus at the outer side of the joint. The tear usually occurs in a twisting injury with the player's foot being fixed to the ground. Forced bending or hyperextension of the knee can also tear the meniscus. Medial meniscus tears and medial collateral ligament injuries often occur together and may be confused with each other. This also applies in some cases of anterior cruciate injury.

There are many types of meniscus tear and in some there may be a mobile fragment of cartilage which gets lodged in the joint, thereby blocking movement. This is called 'locking' and usually occurs with the knee bent and the player being unable to bend or staighten the knee. The 'locking' may be momentary or persist until the leg is gently manipulated (by expert hands) free of the obstruction.

Symptoms are pain at the time of injury, felt at the side of the knee where the meniscus is torn. Locking may occur in the acute situation or can happen repeatedly in the case of an old injury. There is usually tenderness over the joint line (medial or lateral) and a small effusion (fluid) may be present in the joint. Turning the foot inwards or outwards with the knee bent at 90° can bring on the pain at the side of the tear.

Treatment
Rest, ice, compression and elevation will help in the acute situation. Major tears with 'locking' require immediate medical assess-

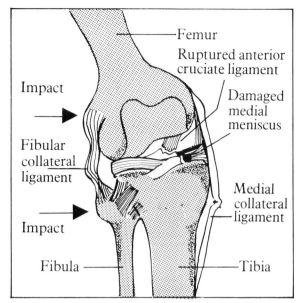

Severe direct impact from the lateral side of the knee causing a rupture of anterior cruciate ligament and medial meniscus tear.

ment. In the past, a torn cartilage involved surgery and removal of the cartilage but this is no longer the case. Partial removal of the torn piec cartilage is often enough and is more desirable since there is evidence to suggest that complete removal of a cartilage (total meniscectomy) may increase the risk of developing degenerative arthritis in later life.

The diagnosis of a torn cartilage is confirmed either by an X-ray with an injection of dye into the joint (arthrography) or more accurately by looking directly inside the joint with a small viewing scope (arthroscopy). Repair, partial removal or total removal of the torn cartilage can then be carried out although more formal surgery may be necessary.

The rehabilitation programme should be started almost immediately in order to prevent weakening and wasting of the thigh muscles, whether surgery takes place or not. Training for sport should not be considered until knee motion is almost normal and the strength of the thigh muscles is adequate.

Loose bodies in the knee (inc. *Osteochondritis dissecans*)

A tear may result in a loose fragment of cartilage floating free within the knee joint.

Another less common cause of a loose body is a condition called Osteochondritis dissecans. This usually affects adolescents and is a condition where a small fragment of bone and cartilage breaks away from the lining of the femur inside the knee joint. The reason for this is unclear. Symptoms are knee pain (usually aching in nature and coming on during or after exercise), variable build-up of fluid in the joint and a history of 'locking'. Diagnosis is made by X-ray.

Treatment

Rest, even if symptoms are mild. Some doctors even recommend a plaster cast to immobilize the knee for a short time. If pain and/or 'locking' continues, then surgical removal of old loose bodies is recommended. Reattachment of the fragment to the femur is possible in some cases (particularly the newer ones). Because of an increased likelihood of degenerative arthritis in later life, it is important to evaluate one's commitment to certain sports and to only return to sport when symptoms have totally disappeared and when muscle strength is good and the knee fully mobile.

Dislocation of the kneecap (*patella*)

A direct blow to one side of the kneecap can cause it to dislocate. This is more likely to happen in people with a prominent or small underdeveloped kneecap and in some cases simply pivoting on a bent knee and then straightening it (as in changing direction) can dislocate the kneecap.

Contact sports are most likely to lead to this injury. The diagnosis is usually obvious with intense pain, immediate swelling of the knee joint, tenderness, loss of movement of the knee and visible displacement of the kneecap. In some cases, the kneecap can dislocate and return to its correct position almost immediately, but here the player has the sensation that his kneecap has 'moved out' and pain and swelling are present.

Treatment

See a doctor as soon as possible. X-rays should be taken, the dislocated kneecap manipulated back and a firm strapping or plaster cast applied. A long course of physiotherapy and rehabilitation is necessary to settle the swelling, improve mobility and build up the quadriceps muscles.

Recurrent dislocations can occur when there is underdevelopment of the kneecap itself or the groove in which it lies on the femur. In these cases, muscle strengthening exercises (straight-leg exercises) are important but surgery may be necessary later on.

Fractures of the patella can also occur after a direct fall onto the kneecap. These range from hairline cracks to displaced fractures and treatment varies accordingly from simple strapping to a plaster cast for 3-4 weeks, or surgical repair.

X-ray of transverse fracture of the patella which can be caused by a fall or a blow to the kneecap.

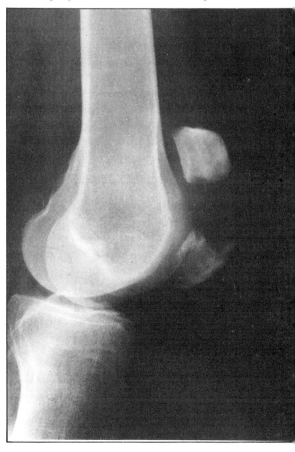

Jumper's knee (*Patellar tendon injuries*)

The patellar tendon is the broad, strong tendon that runs from the kneecap down onto the upper part of the shinbone (tibia). It is really an extension of the tendon of the quadriceps muscles and is used in straight-

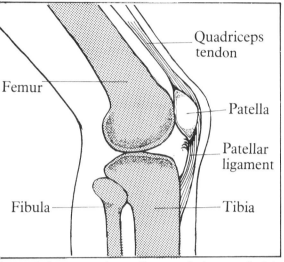

Jumper's knee: note the small tear at the lower end of the patella where it is attached to the patellar tendon.

ning (as in kicking or jumping) the knee or supporting the leg with the knee bent. Injuries here can vary from an acute tear to a chronic overuse strain or tendinitis. These injuries occur in 'jumping' sports such as basketball, volleyball and, of course, high, triple and long jumping. They are also seen in weight-lifters, badminton or squash players where high-impact loading on a bent knee occurs.

In acute tears, pain is sudden but, in overuse strain, it comes on gradually during or after exercise. There is local tenderness over the tendon which is most common just at the lower border of the knee-cap. Pain is reproduced by standing on and bending the affected leg or kicking out against resistance.

Treatment
Ice and rest for 48 hours with gentle weight-bearing and heat after this period. If symptoms are severe, anti-inflammatory medication may be prescribed by a doctor. Ultrasound and gentle stretching are recommended after pain has settled, then flexibility training followed by strengthening of the quadriceps muscle.

Osgood-Schlatter's disease

This is a condition of adolescence and usually affects boys. There is inflammation and slight separation at the attachment of the patellar tendon to the bony prominence on the upper front part of the tibia (tibial tuberosity). It appears to be an overuse injury aggravated, particularly, by kicking. Pain and tenderness are localized and there may be visible swelling. Straightening the leg against resistance brings on the pain. An X-ray will often show changes in the bone at this point.

Treatment
Rest, followed by heat applied to the site of the injury. Avoidance of aggravating activities is usually required for a lengthy period and it may be necessary to change sports, albeit temporarily. This condition will cure itself and does not occur after the bone has stopped growing at about 17 years of age.

Bursitis

There are several sacs of fluid (bursae) around the knee that can be damaged by impact or overuse, causing inflammation and swelling. A typical example is 'housemaid's knee' where the bursa in front of the kneecap becomes inflamed as a result of prolonged

In Osgood-Schlatter's disease, constant traction where the patellar tendon is attached to the tibia leads to inflammation and separation of the growing bone here.

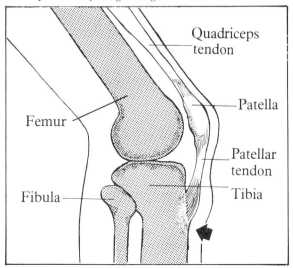

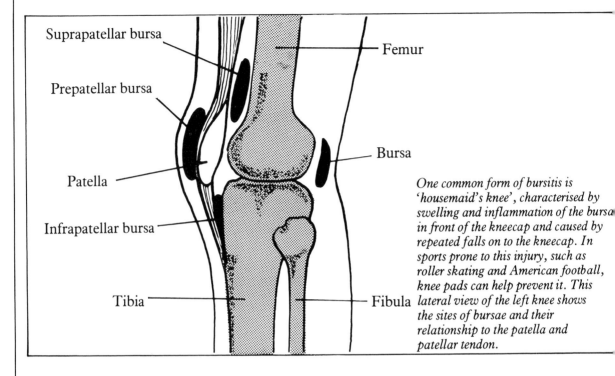

Suprapatellar bursa

Prepatellar bursa

Patella

Infrapatellar bursa

Tibia

Femur

Bursa

Fibula

One common form of bursitis is 'housemaid's knee', characterised by swelling and inflammation of the bursa in front of the kneecap and caused by repeated falls on to the kneecap. In sports prone to this injury, such as roller skating and American football, knee pads can help prevent it. This lateral view of the left knee shows the sites of bursae and their relationship to the patella and patellar tendon.

or repeated kneeling. In sport, repeated falls onto the kneecap can produce a similar condition.

Treatment
Rest, ice, compression and elevation, followed by local heat after 24-48 hours. Rest is essential until the pain has settled. Wearing protective knee guards will prevent a recurrence in high-risk sports such as roller-skating, American football or ice hockey. Large swellings may be drained by a doctor with a needle.

Runner's knee *(Ilio-tibial band friction syndrome)*

The ilio-tibial band is a tendon-like band of tissue which runs down from a muscle at the upper outer part of the thigh. It attaches just below the knee at the outer side of the leg. As the knee bends and straightens, this band slips to and fro across the lower end of the femur at a bony point (the epicondyle). Inflammation at this point is most likely to occur in long-distance runners, especially those who have hyperpronation of their fee or run on inclines and uneven ground because of the repetitive sliding motion. A with other overuse injuries, this can become a chronic problem if it is not picked up early Pain usually comes on during running. The more it is aggravated, the sooner it comes or in a run. Pain is felt at one point (usually 20-30° of flexion) as the knee is bent and straightened and a 'click' may be felt. Tenderness is often present.

Treatment
Ice at first. Rest from running is essentia followed by ultrasound, stretching an strengthening exercises when pain an tenderness has settled. Orthotics are necessary to correct hyperpronation of the feet Chronic cases may require a steroid injectio from the doctor. Surgery is a last resort.

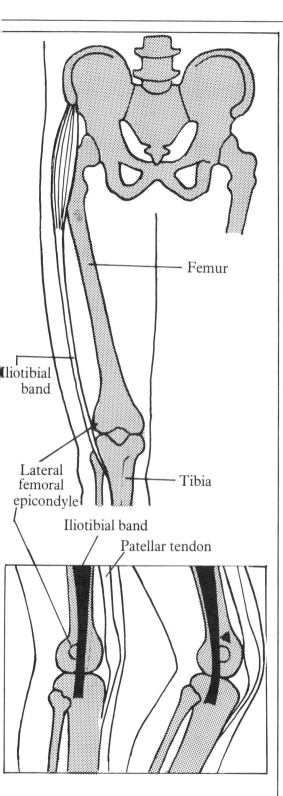

Femur

Iliotibial
band

Lateral
femoral
epicondyle

Tibia

Iliotibial band

Patellar tendon

Runner's knee is the most common cause of knee pain in runners. This lateral view of the right knee shows that as the knee bends to 20-30°, the fibrous band slides across the lateral femoral epicondyle. Overuse can lead to inflammation at this point.

Lower leg injuries

Fractures

Fractures of the tibia and fibula are most common in Alpine skiers and contact sports. These injuries require immediate medical attention. Any injury where there is marked bony tenderness or swelling, inability to move an injured leg, or severe pain should be seen by the doctor. If there is any doubt that there may be a fracture, then a cautionary X-ray is appropriate.

Stress fractures

These can occur in either the tibia or fibula and are usually the result of repeated loading on the bone due to excessive running or jumping. Runners are those usually affected but other sportsmen are at risk – for example Imran Khan, the Sussex and Pakistan test cricketer, suffered a stress fracture. High-mileage is not a prerequisite for these small hairline cracks at one side of the bone, and as little as 10-15 miles per week can cause them. The tibia is usually affected at the junction of its upper two-thirds whereas the fibula is more often affected at its lower end just above the ankle. The athlete usually complains of shin pain or soreness during or after a run, which gradually becomes more severe and more frequent as he or she continues to train at the usual level. This pain will settle with rest but recur as running is resumed. Localized tenderness over the bone is common and occasionally there is slight swelling. Confusion with 'shin splints' is common. X-rays tend to show no abnormality at first but a repeat X-ray 2-4 weeks later may show the fracture. If a stress fracture is strongly suspected or if an athlete has persistent unexplained shin pain, then the doctor can arrange a bone scan which will confirm the diagnosis. Another useful test is the application of ultrasound by the physiotherapist directly over the bone. In the case of a stress fracture, this will often induce quite intense pain at that site. The main clues to the diagnosis are the history of increasing shin pain with running and

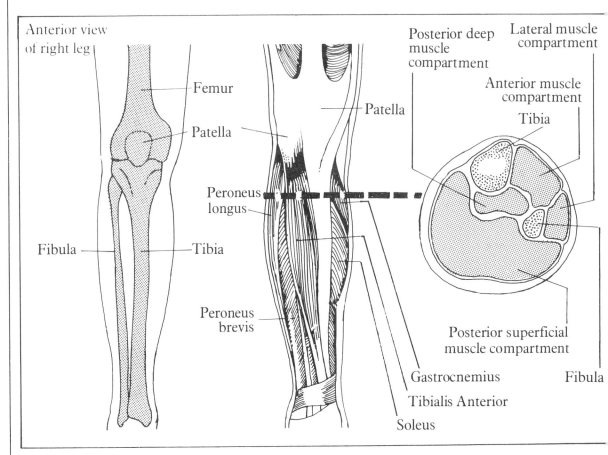

Anterior view of right leg

Femur

Patella

Fibula

Tibia

Peroneus longus

Peroneus brevis

Patella

Peroneus longus

Posterior deep muscle compartment

Lateral muscle compartment

Anterior muscle compartment

Tibia

Posterior superficial muscle compartment

Gastrocnemius

Fibula

Tibialis Anterior

Soleus

localized tenderness directly over the bone.

Treatment

Rest and avoidance of all activities which involve jumping or running. No other treatment is necessary. Tibial stress fractures require about 8-10 weeks for healing and fibular stress fractures require about six weeks. During this time it is essential to avoid a premature return to running, despite the absence of pain and symptoms, as delayed healing will result. A plaster cast may be required for very painful fractures or where healing is delayed and the state of the fracture should be checked before returning to running. Cycling and swimming are good forms of exercise for maintaining conditioning during this period of rest from running.

Compartment syndromes

The muscles in the lower leg run longitudin-

ally and are divided into four separate compartments by tough, thin layers of connective tissue which are attached to the tibia and fibula and the tissue just below the skin. There are, in effect, four compartments running lengthwise along the leg between the knee and ankle which contain the muscles, blood vessels and nerves in the leg. The layers surrounding the individual compartments are tight and inelastic and therefore any swelling inside a compartment will cause a rise in pressure which, in turn, compresses the muscles, nerves and blood vessels. This causes symptoms such as pain, tenderness, weakness and even numbness in the leg and foot. This condition is called 'compartment syndrome'.

Acute compartment syndrome

A direct blow to the leg (as in a kick in foot

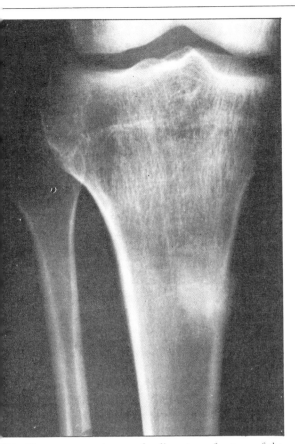

This X-ray picture shows a healing stress fracture of the shaft of the tibia.

ball or rugby) can cause bleeding inside a compartment which will lead to this pressure rise and its associated symptoms. Acute muscle tears have the same results. However, the most common cause of an acute compartment syndrome is overuse, resulting from excessive training or running, particularly on a hard surface, without adequate preparation. The anterior compartment is the one usually involved and road runners are at greatest risk. Symptoms are acute pain felt over the front of the leg coming on with running and increasing until the activity is stopped. There may be weakness and difficulty in bending the foot upwards, and numbness in the lower leg or foot can be felt. The muscles to the outer (lateral) side of the shinbone are usually tender and may be swollen. Pain is brought on by bending the foot downwards.

Treatment: Rest followed by ice and elevation. If pain is severe and does not settle or if numbness persists, then a doctor should be seen as the artery in the front of the leg may be compressed, thereby cutting off the blood supply to part of the foot and leg.

Chronic compartment syndrome

In endurance athletes, chronic anterior compartment syndrome can be caused by continued running or walking. These people develop an increased muscle bulk in the front part of their leg and the increase in blood flow during exercise can lead to this build up of pressure. The muscles, being starved of oxygen, begin to ache and eventually lose power so that the person is unable to continue running or walking. Rest settles the pain, but it recurs if activity is resumed too soon. Again, muscle tenderness, swelling, weakness and numbness may all be present.

Posterior compartment syndrome also occurs in chronic form and gives rise to pain and soreness at the inner and posterior surface of the tibia. Runners and jumpers are affected mainly and this time pain is felt on 'take-off' or standing on tip-toe.

Treatment: Rest, plus reduction in the level of training for both anterior and posterior compartment syndrome. A change in running surface, footwear or even technique may help. Chronic persistent cases may require surgery to enlarge the affected compartment, giving the muscles more space.

Shin splints *(Medial tibial stress syndrome; periostitis)*

This term is often used to describe 'shin soreness' in the athlete or sportsman and can be confused with a stress fracture, compartment syndrome or even inflammation of one of the tendons in the front of the lower leg. True shin splints is due to inflammation at the point of attachment of one of the muscles in the lower leg to the bone (periostitis). Some people do speak of anterior, posterior or lateral shin splints according to the site of inflammation and the muscles affected. The most common site, however, is at the lower, inner part of the tibia (medial tibial stress syndrome). This can happen in many different sports where running or jumping on hard surfaces is necessary. Running (track, road or cross-country), long-jump, triple-jump, hurdling, dancing and aerobics are frequent causes. Running technique, foot-wear and running surface are all important factors. However, it is not just hard surfaces that are responsible – a change in running surface, such as from track to cross-country, may also cause shin splints. Those people who run with their toes pointing out or who run on their toes (as opposed to heel-to-toe) or people with flat feet or a high instep can be affected. Spiked shoes or boots on a hard surface also increase the likelihood of getting shin splints. Aerobics teachers or regular class students who perform on a hard floor (especially in bare feet) are particularly at risk.

Symptoms are pain felt at the inner margin of the lower half of the tibia (of one or both legs), with associated tenderness. Swelling is not uncommon but usually only slight. Pain is directly related to running or jumping and gradually eases with rest. Tenderness is normally felt over a reasonably large area and not directly over the front of the bone but to the side of it. This is helpful in distinguishing shin splins from a stress fracture, where tenderness is often much more localised and over the bone itself.

Treatment

If symptoms do not recur after a reasonable period of rest (7-10 days) shin splints, rather than stress fracture, is the probable cause of the injury. In the first instance, rest early on is essential. Ice, followed by local heat and ultrasound is beneficial with a gradual return to activity only after all symptoms have disappeared. Chronic cases may benefit from carefully administered steroid injections but rest after injection is imperative. Swimming and cycling (pedalling with the heel rather than the toe) can be used to maintain fitness. Changing to a softer running surface or changing shoes may help prevent a recurrence while orthotics for flat-feet is advisable. A cutting back in activity and then a gradual build-up in frequency and intensity is recommended.

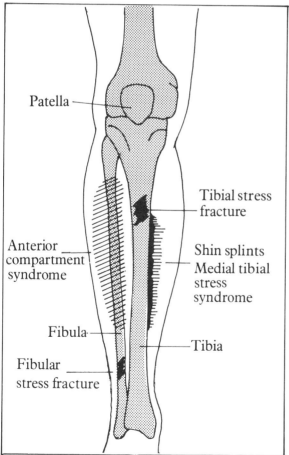

This anterior view of the right leg shows the common sites of shin pain in runners. Overtraining and road-running may contribute to shin splints and stress fractures.

Patella

Tibial stress fracture

Anterior compartment syndrome

Shin splints
Medial tibial stress syndrome

Fibula

Tibia

Fibular stress fracture

Calf strain (*Tennis leg*)

The two major muscles in the calf, the gastrocnemius (superficial) and the soleus (deep) are frequently strained in sports where there is a lot of jumping or thrusting off one foot. Examples are court games such as squash, badminton, racquet-ball, basketball, volleyball and tennis, or the hurdling and jumping events in athletics. At their lower end, these muscles attach into the heel bone (calcaneum) via the Achilles tendon and are important for the leverage of take-off from the ground, as well as the shock ab-

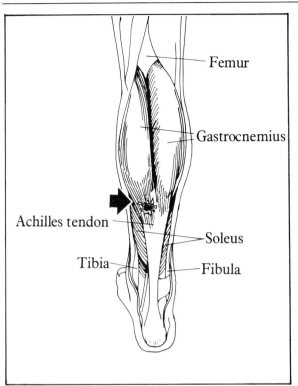

This illustrates a partial tear of the gastrocnemius muscle at the lower part of the muscle belly.

sorption of landing. Small tears or ruptures in the muscle belly can be caused by either of these abrupt actions and may occur at any point along the muscle.

Symptoms of calf strain include pain in the calf (suddenly in the case of a tear and gradually coming on in a more chronic strain), tenderness in the calf muscle itself, and swelling or even bruising in the more severe tears. Pain is felt on standing on tip-toe.

Treatment
Rest, ice, compression and elevation followed, after 48 hours, by gentle stretching with local heat application and a gradual return to training. More severe tears may require medical attention and in a few cases a surgical repair may be considered. Inadequate rehabilitation, with either a lack of gentle stretching or a too-rapid return to sport and a recurrence of the injury, can lead to scarring within the muscle and this in turn makes repeated tears more likely.

Plantaris rupture

This is a small muscle which lies deep in the calf and which can rupture in activities where sprinting or sharp changes in direction take place (i.e. on the soccer or rugby field). It is also injured in those sports where calf strains can occur. The onset of pain is typically acute and the person may feel as if they have been struck in the back of the leg – with sometimes an associated sound like a muffled gunshot (less dramatic than in Achilles ruptures). Symptoms are similar to those for a calf strain or small Achilles tear with a feeling of pain deep in the mid-calf region.

Treatment
This is the same as for calf strain although surgical repair is never necessary as this muscle is not used for normal leg function.

Achilles tendon injuries

Achilles tendon rupture

This may be a complete or partial rupture and occurs mainly, as with calf strain, in court games, as well as hurdling and jumping events in athletics.

Total rupture: The diagnosis of this is fairly straightforward. The person feels a sudden snap in the tendon or often describes it like being kicked or hit by a blow in the back of the leg. There may be a loud 'snap' like a gunshot. Pain is instantaneous but may settle somewhat and there is swelling around the tendon and tenderness in this region. A gap may be felt in this tendon, weakness is present and the injured person is unable to stand on tip-toe on the affected foot. If the person lies on his or her stomach and the calf muscle is squeezed, the foot will not move downwards, as it does on the unaffected side.

Treatment: Medical attention is necessary as surgical repair of the ruptured tendon should be carried out as soon as possible. After the operation, a plaster cast is worn for about six weeks and, following this, a prolonged period of rehabilitation is necessary to regain full mobility of the leg and ankle before strength training is commenced.

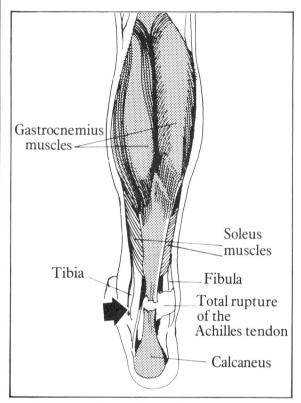

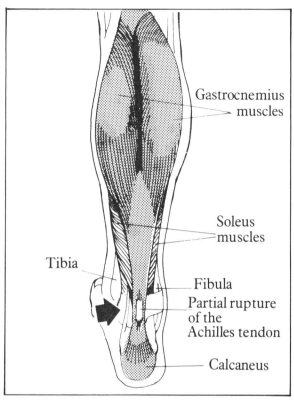

Total rupture of the Achilles tendon prohibits the person from standing on tip-toe.

This illustration shows a partial rupture of the Achilles tendon which requires quick treatment.

Return to sport is usually slow and a break of six months is not unusual.

Partial rupture: The symptoms of partial rupture of the Achilles tendon are less dramatic, although the initial onset of pain is usually sudden. Depending on the size of the rupture, there is local swelling, tenderness, with accompanying weakness and pain when standing on tip-toe. In small tears, the person may be unaware of the importance of the injury and may continue to play sport or train, with the result that increasing pain and stiffness is felt after activity until he or she is unable to continue.

Treatment: In minor ruptures or strains, rest and ice with crutches to prevent weight-bearing, followed by physiotherapy and a gentle, prolonged rehabilitation programme. More severe ruptures may require the appli-

cation of a plaster cast for 3-4 weeks, followed by rehabilitation. Surgical repair is often considered for the more severe partial ruptures or when small repeated ruptures have led to focal degeneration of part of the tendon. Full recovery will only occur if aggravating activities are introduced slowly into the rehabilitation programme. Swimming is to be encouraged as a means of maintaining fitness.

Achilles tendinitis or peritendinitis

This is the most common type of Achilles tendon injury and can affect almost any sportsman involved in running or jumping. It is a type of overuse injury and can result from excessive training or activity. Factors contributing to this injury are inadequate warm up and stretching prior to exercise, running on very soft surfaces (e.g. sand) or very hard surfaces, running uphill, and wearing shoes with poor shock-absorption qualities or a very flat, low heel. Others also prone to this injury are runners with flat feet or an exaggerated heel-to-toe running gait, sportsmen who exercise in cold weather, and women who regularly wear high heels and do not stretch adequately prior to exercise. The symptoms are pain in the region of the Achilles tendon, tenderness and diffuse swelling over the tendon. A 'creaking' sensation may be felt over the tendon on bending the ankle up and down. There is usually stiffness and pain on the following morning after exercise. People often find that the pain and stiffness settle with exercise and therefore continue to aggravate the tendon by not resting adequately.

Treatment
Rest is essential. Ice is recommended in the acute phase, followed later by heat and ultrasound. A heel pad should be worn to raise the heel (about 1 cm/1⅜ inches) and take the strain off the injured tendon. When the pain and swelling has settled, gentle stretching and mobility exercises can be started, followed later by strengthening and a gradual return to activity.

Many acute cases are not rested for long enough and the return to sport is too rapid. This leads to a chronic condition which can be very difficult to treat and which may require a complete break from sport. Surgery is only carried out in the most persistent cases where there is a lot of scar tissue. Injections of steroid around this tendon carry the very real risk of tendon rupture, particularly if the athlete fails to rest after this form of treatment.

Preventative measures are heel raises on shoes or heel wedges in running shoes, adequate static stretching exercises before and after exercise, and rest at the first sign of a recurrence of symptoms.

Pump bump *(Achilles or calcaneal bursitis)*

Many runners notice a swelling at the back of the heel bone just below and behind the point of attachment of the Achilles tendon. This is due to swelling of a small sac of fluid (bursa) that lies here and which is aggravated by the pressure of running shoes around the heel. The surrounding skin is often red and pain is felt on running on hills or inclines. There may be tenderness of this swelling.

Treatment
This is by relieving the pressure on this area. Wearing shoes without backs is recommended (e.g. clogs, sandals or open slippers). Pressure can be relieved by applying a doughnut-shaped pad around the inflamed region. Rest from running until symptoms settle and then review of the heel counters of the running shoes can prevent a recurrence.

Sever's disease *(Apophysitis calcanei)*

In active adolescents, continued traction at the point of attachment of the Achilles tendon to the heel bone caused by running and jumping, can lead to inflammation and fragmentation of this growing area of bone. Symptoms are heel pain with local tenderness at the back of the heel. X-ray changes are typical.

Treatment
Rest until the symptoms have settled and use a heel raise or wedge to reduce the strain on the Achilles tendon. This condition will settle completely once the bone fuses and growth ceases at around 17 years of age.

Deep retrocalcaneal bursa – a further bursa lies superficially behind the Achilles (pump bump).

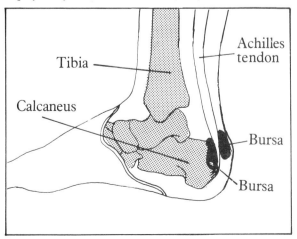

Tibia

Calcaneus

Achilles tendon

Bursa

Bursa

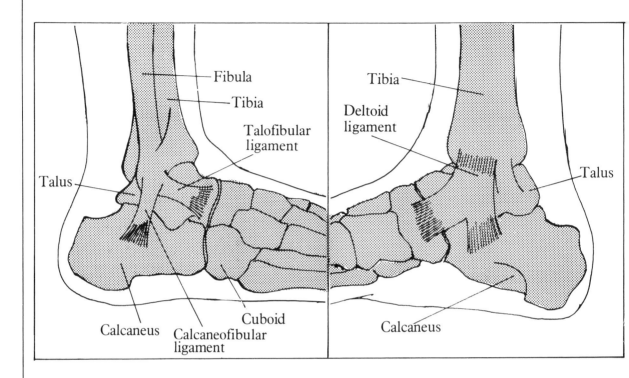

Fibula

Tibia

Talofibular ligament

Talus

Calcaneus

Calcaneofibular ligament

Cuboid

Tibia

Deltoid ligament

Talus

Calcaneus

Ankle injuries

The ankle joint is a mortice joint between the two bones of the leg (tibia and fibula) and a large bone in the foot (talus). It is supported by a joint capsule and by strong ligaments on either side. The entire weight of the body is borne through the ankle joint in standing, running and jumping and a strong, stable ankle is important for most sports. Injuries are extremely common and can occur in any sport but more particularly in contact sports such as rugby, football, American football, ball sports such as basketball, netball, volleyball, handball, court games and skiing. 'Turning over' one's ankle can occur at any time, especially on uneven ground or when landing from a height, or when tripping or being tackled. Ankle injuries are usually twisting injuries, where the foot is turned inwards or outwards and forced by impact or the person's own weight beyond the limits of normal movement. The severity of injury varies according to the force of impact or degree of twisting force. Minor sprains of

the ankle ligaments are most common but a more severe injury can lead to ankle ligament rupture (partial or total) and/or ankle fractures.

Ankle fractures

These usually only happen in a severe twisting injury. A small piece of the bone may be torn off from the end of the tibia or fibula, or a more definite fracture at the lower end of one of these bones can occur. Swelling is considerable and standing on the foot usually causes severe pain. If there is severe pain and swelling with tenderness directly over the bone, then an X-ray should be arranged.

Treatment
If there is no displacement of the fracture and the ankle is stable, a plaster cast is usually applied for about six weeks. Any displacement or instability of the ankle joint will require an operation to either manipulate the bones back into place or to fix them in place with a pin. A plaster cast is applied after the operation. Rehabilitation is es-

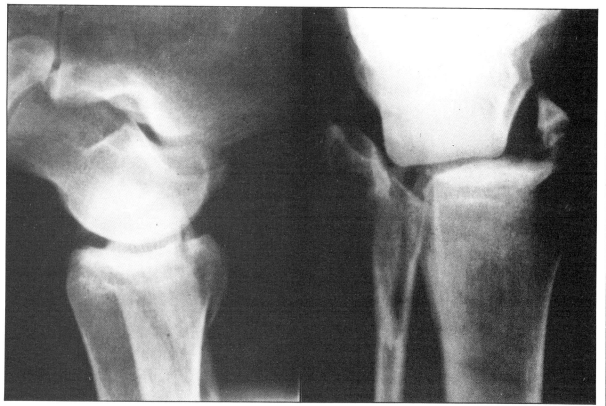

X-rays of a fractured ankle, usually caused by severe twisting. Prolonged rehabilitation, including wobble-board exercises, is essential to regain mobility of the joint.

sential after removal of the plaster to regain full mobility of the ankle and to build up the leg muscles. Proprioceptive exercises (wobbleboard exercises) are important and it will usually be 3-4 months before full training can be resumed.

Ankle ligament injuries

The type and extent of ligament damage will be determined by the direction and force of the injury. The most common type is an inversion sprain, where the foot is forcibly turned inwards with the athlete's weight going 'over' the ankle, thereby stretching and tearing the ligament on the outside of the joint (lateral ligament). An eversion injury, where the foot is turned outwards, leads to a medial ligament sprain on the inside of the ankle. Severe injuries are often a combination of medial and lateral ligament sprain or rupture, occasionally with a fracture of one or both of the ankle bones. The capsule (or lining) of the ankle joint may also be stretched or torn in this sort of injury and this usually gives rise to bleeding into the

ankle joint itself.

Symptoms of an ankle ligament injury are acute pain at the time of the injury, swelling, tenderness, bruising and pain on standing. In minor sprains, it is often possible to 'run through' this initial pain and continue the game. In other cases, pain is severe and standing on or moving the foot becomes unbearable. Swelling can come on quickly or build up over several hours. Bruising is common. Tenderness and swelling occur over the site of the injury and any movement which stretches and stresses the injured ligament is painful. If there is a lot of swelling and yet the foot can be twisted firmly without much pain in the direction of the injury (i.e. inwards in a lateral ligament injury), a complete rupture of the ligament should be suspected. Any evidence of excessive movement at the ankle joint suggests instability, particularly when the foot or heel is pulled forward while stabilizing the tibia. A doctor should be seen if a fracture or ligament rupture is suspected or with any severe ankle sprain when there is bony tenderness,

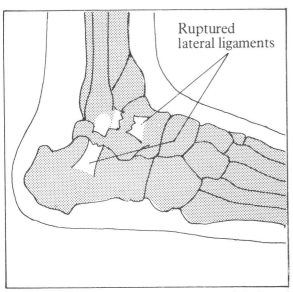

This illustration shows a complete rupture of the lateral ligaments in the ankle.

marked swelling or bruising, or evidence of instability.

Treatment

Immediate rest, ice, compression and elevation for 48 hours. In cases of partial ligament rupture with considerable swelling, strapping may be recommended for anything up to three weeks. However, in most cases of ankle sprain, mobility exercises and gentle weight-bearing should be commenced early on. Anti-inflammatory drugs may be prescribed by the doctor and after 48 hours, heat and ultrasound can be used. The rehabilitation programme has to be tailored to the severity of the injury. Complete ligament ruptures require immediate surgical repair in the young, active athlete although immobilization in a plaster cast for about six weeks is an alternative treatment. Partial ruptures require an initial period of immobilization followed by intensive physiotherapy. Most ankle sprains heal with 1-3 weeks of treatment. During the rehabilitation period, balancing exercises are carried out on a 'wobble-board' to improve the position sense around the ankle and this helps the muscles to contract early to prevent the ankle going 'over' again. Standing and bal-

ancing on an upturned metal dustbin-lid is a simple way of carrying out these exercises at home. Strengthening exercises can be started when there is full mobility with no pain. It is important to treat all ankle injuries with respect. Adequate mobility, balancing and strengthening exercises should be carried out prior to a return to sport.

The rehabilitation programme for ankle ligament injuries can stretch over many weeks. This is important, however, in order to prevent chronic scarring or stretching of the ligaments which can give rise to pain and instability.

Strapping can be worn to try and protect the ankle during sport. The simplest type of strapping is a U-shaped stirrup of adhesive sports-tape running under the heel and up each side of the ankle with a few circular bands (not too tight) around the upper ends to keep the stirrup in place. There is a view that such strapping restricts movement and is therefore likely to create excessive forces about the player's knee and leg. However, as most players soon find out, after 10-15 minutes of exercise the tape tends to loosen and it works not so much by joint restriction but by helping to reinforce the joint position sense. This encourages the relevant muscles to contract early to prevent the ankle twisting over. In American and Australian professional football, strapping is worn by the majority of players to prevent ankle injuries and there is no evidence that they suffer more leg injuries as a result.

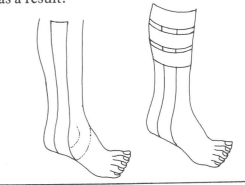

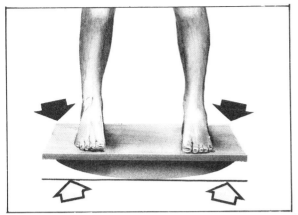

A wobble-board is supported on two concave pieces of wood and helps increase ankle mobility after an injury.

Footballer's ankle

Repeated stretching of the front of the ankle joint capsule (e.g. in kicking or sliding on a down-turned ankle during soccer games) causes this condition, which is characterised by small bony outgrowths (osteophytes) at the site of attachment of the capsule to the front of the ankle joint. A similar condition can arise from constant impact on the bones at this point in people who do a lot of hill climbing or running (where the foot is forced upwards against the front of the ankle). Symptoms include pain at the front of the ankle on bending the foot down or pulling it right up, pain after vigorous running or kicking a ball, stiffness and loss of mobility of the ankle and sometimes tenderness. An X-ray will show the bony outgrowth.

Treatment

Rest during the acute stages followed by mobility and strength training with gentle stretching. Surgery to remove the bony tissue may be offered if other measures fail. In many cases of chronic pain, continued sporting activity will only aggravate this condition and the person should be advised that a change in sport may be necessary in order to avoid further damage.

Tibialis posterior tendinitis

The tibialis posterior is a muscle that lies deep in the calf behind the tibia and fibula and which runs into a tendon which then passes behind the ankle joint at the inside of the foot before attaching to a bone at the inner side of the instep. This tendon may become inflamed with overuse in runners, particularly when they have pronated or flat feet. Pain is felt just behind and below the ankle on the inner (medial) side during exercise. Tenderness and occasionally swelling is present. 'Creaking' may be felt as the tendon is moved.

Treatment

Rest, ice, compression and elevation, followed by heat and a gentle return to exercise. In chronic cases, anti-inflammatory tablets or a steroid injection may be given by the doctor. Arch supports are important in pronated or flat feet. Exercises should not be resumed until symptoms have settled.

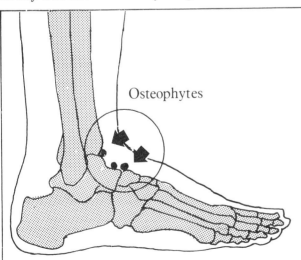
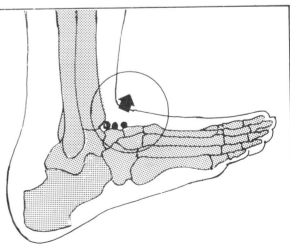

Osteophytes

In footballer's ankle, repeated stretching or impact at the front of the ankle joint leads to degenerative changes and small bony outgrowths (osteophytes) which impinge against each other when the foot is raised (right).

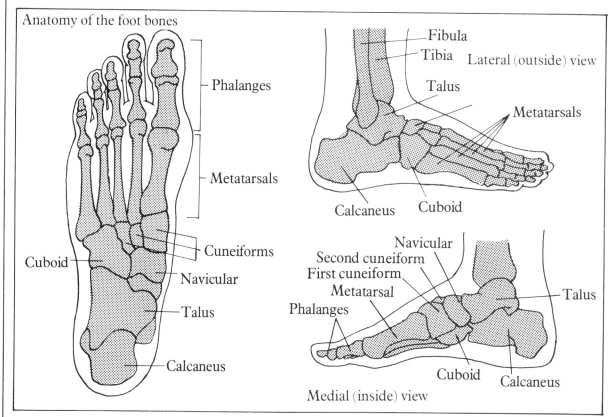

Anatomy of the foot bones

Phalanges

Metatarsals

Cuboid

Cuneiforms

Navicular

Talus

Calcaneus

Fibula

Tibia — Lateral (outside) view

Talus

Metatarsals

Calcaneus — Cuboid

Navicular

Second cuneiform

First cuneiform

Metatarsal

Phalanges

Talus

Cuboid — Calcaneus

Medial (inside) view

Foot injuries

The foot is a complex structure of small bones, ligaments, muscles and their tendons, which support the body when standing, running or jumping. Considerable loads are imparted to the ground through the foot and sports which involve a lot of running and jumping may cause overloading on one or more of these structures. The normal anatomy of the foot is designed to transmit these forces effectively. Any variation in the normal anatomical alignment of the bones in the foot (i.e. any pre-existing deformity) can create extra stresses leading to an overuse injury. Poor running technique or inadequate equipment may also create overloading.

Hyperpronated or flat foot

This has already been mentioned in associ-ation with a variety of lower limb overuse injuries. In a normal foot, as it lands on the ground, the outer side touches first and then, as the weight is carried over on to the leg, the inner side of the foot comes onto the ground. There is a slight rotation of the foot (pronation) to allow this to happen. The arch of the foot acts as a shock-absorber and gives way slightly to let the foot hug the contours of the ground to some extent. In the flat-foot or hyperpronated foot, the arch collapses right down and this allows the foot to pronate further, thereby pressing more of the inner side of the foot onto the ground. In other words, the sole of the foot is forced against the ground by this excess pronation. The hyperpronated foot also throws more strain onto other structures in the foot and also slightly alters the angle of forces in the leg (hence the strain onto the knee, forcing it to rotate inwards). Injuries associated with the hyperpronated foot are patello-femoral syndrome, plantar fasciitis, tibialis posterior tenditis, Achilles tendinitis and foot strain.

Treatment

Adequate arch support in shoes is essential. Intrinsic muscle foot exercises (e.g. by picking up pencils with the toes) may help to strengthen the relevant muscles although the anatomical structures will not change. Other anatomical deformities which may cause problems in the feet include a high-arched foot (pes cavus), bunions (hallux valgus) or a shortened big toe (Morton's foot). Any difference in leg length can also create foot strain and should be corrected by means of a heel or shoe raise on the side of the shortened leg.

Plantar fasciitis (*Policeman's heel*)

The plantar fascia is a tough band of tissue that bridges the sole of the foot from the front of the bottom of the heel forwards to the ball of the foot (the metatarsal arch). It helps to stabilize and support the instep (longitudinal arch) of the foot. During take-off, the plantar fascia is stretched as the toes are bent upwards, and athletes who run a lot on hard surfaces, or in stiff-soled shoes, may get an overuse strain on this fascia. People with flat feet are more likely to suffer from this. An acute strain can occur with a sudden, sharp take-off or change in direction. Pain is felt at the attachment of this fascia to the bottom of the heel (on its inner side). This area is tender and the person may walk on tip-toe to ease the pain. X-rays often show a little bony outgrowth here (bony spur) but this is often found in people without pain.

Treatment

Rest by taking the weight off the heel or using a cushioned heel insert (with an area cut out to fit under the tender spot). Ultrasound may help. Steroid injections are useful in persistent cases but rest afterwards is essential to prevent ruptures of the fascia. Gentle stretching exercises can be started once the pain settles. Shoe modification is recommended, to correct any underlying hyperpronation and to provide adequate shock absorption.

Metatarsal stress fractures (*March fracture*)

Stress fractures are quite common along the shaft of one of the metatarsal bones in the

Metatarsal stress fractures in runners and other athletes are usually caused by over-training.

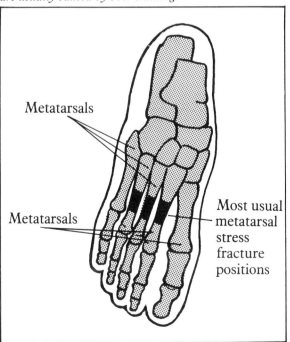

Metatarsals

Metatarsals

Most usual metatarsal stress fracture positions

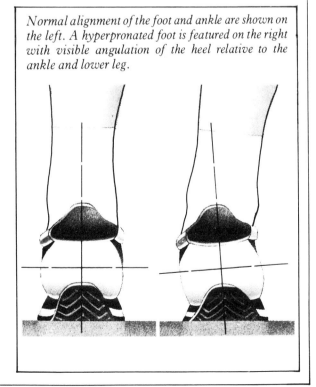

Normal alignment of the foot and ankle are shown on the left. A hyperpronated foot is featured on the right with visible angulation of the heel relative to the ankle and lower leg.

centre of the foot and occur as a direct result of excessive training, in runners and athletes particularly. Pain comes on during running or even walking, and there is localized tenderness, often with associated swelling, over the mid-portion of the foot. An X-ray may show a fracture but if not – and a fracture is strongly suspected (or if pain does not settle) – then the X-ray should be repeated two weeks later. A bone scan is a more accurate test.

Treatment
Rest from sport for 4-6 weeks. Healing of the fracture should be confirmed on X-ray before training is resumed.

Tenosynovitis

A variety of tendons in the foot can become inflamed from overuse or ill-fitting shoes. A common site is on the top of the foot where the tendons responsible for straightening the toes can get irritated by tight boot or shoe laces.

Treatment
Relief of pressure, rest and shoe adjustment to prevent a recurrence (soft foam padding with a hollow over the inflamed area is useful).

The tibialis posterior tendon behind the ankle can be irritated by overuse in flat-footed runners.

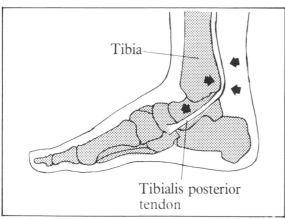

Tibia

Tibialis posterior tendon

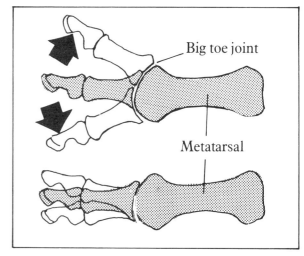

Big toe joint

Metatarsal

Hallux rigidus is characterised by a loss of mobility of the big toe joint in the ball of the foot.

Hallux rigidus *(stiff toe)*

The joint at the base of the big toe (first metatarsophalangeal joint) can become stiff and lose mobility as a result of repeated minor injuries, or simply of its own accord. As the joint stiffens, the rest of the foot has to compensate for this during walking and running and the result can be overuse strains such as plantar fasciitis. The symptoms are pain and stiffness of the big toe and difficulty with bending the toe upwards.

Treatment
Initially, this should be to settle inflammation by rest and anti-inflammatory medication. Later, physiotherapy is needed to return the mobility of the big toe to normal, if possible. If the problem becomes chronic, then shoe adjustments can provide better support and some relief (eg., a bar running across under the ball of the foot either inside or outside the shoe).

Fractures of the toes

These occur in kicking and contact sports. Pain, tenderness and swelling occur at the site of the fracture.

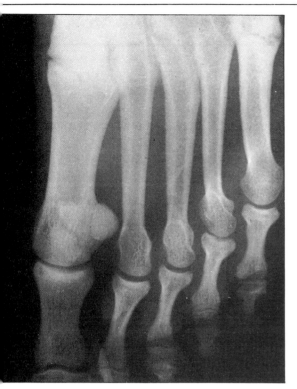

This X-ray photograph shows a fracture of the second toe requiring pain relief only.

Treatment

Simply rest from activity for three to four weeks unless there is displacement of the bones, in which case manipulation and a plaster cast may be necessary.

Metatarsalgia

This is a common condition affecting many runners and sportsmen and women. Pain under the ball of the foot occurs and is due to ligament strain around the joints here. Hard surfaces and thin-soled shoes increase the risk of this occurring.

Treatment

This is simple – rest and a review of the running surface and footwear.

Footwear and foot care

Ill-fitting shoes are responsible for many minor foot problems such as bunions, blisters, bruised toe nails ('turf' toe), foot strain and ingrowing toe nails. Care should be taken to select shoes carefully and to treat these problems early to prevent chronic infection or pain. Runners in particular are prone to foot disorders and running shoes should be tailored to the individual to lessen the risk of these developing.

General first aid

Wounds

All wounds should be cleaned thoroughly with cold water to remove all dirt.
To stop bleeding:
Elevate the limb or affected part. Apply direct local pressure and then apply a pressure bandage. Application of cold is useful (not over fingers or toes).

Abrasions and friction burns

These should be cleaned thoroughly and covered with a dry, sterile dressing to prevent infection. Dressings should be changed daily and the wound aired when possible.

Infections

Any wound which suggests infection, i.e. increasing pain, swelling, tenderness or redness of the skin, needs to be treated by a doctor. All athletes should be actively immunized against tetanus as grass wounds carry with them the risk of tetanus infection. Booster doses of vaccine may be necessary in the case of a dirty wound when the immunization status is not up to date.

Blisters

These can be quite painful and disabling and care should be taken to prevent infection if the skin is broken. Prevention is by means of well-fitting shoes, socks and good hygiene.

CHAPTER THREE

SELF-HELP

It is not always easy to find a doctor or a physiotherapist when you need one. Most sports injuries happen at weekends and the emergency services are not particularly interested unless the injury is really serious and it is usually only several days later that you are able to make an appointment. Not every doctor or physiotherapist wants, or knows enough, to treat sports injuries, which are, by medical standards, fairly trivial conditions that would heal up anyway if they are left alone.

Injury is inescapably linked with sport. Happily, the great majority are relatively minor and, with a little intelligent advice or instruction about how you can help yourself, will heal quite satisfactorily in the minimum of time. The problems come if for want of the right advice or simply because you did not know better, a simple injury becomes a chronic recurring nuisance.

Ideally, every class or sports association should appoint a medical officer or physiotherapist as an advisor, but until that happens, or for those thousands who do not belong to any organisation, a little self help can work wonders.

Understanding your own body

The first step is self knowledge and one of the best ways of learning a little more about your body is by taking a course in first aid. Not only will it teach you about the way that you work, it will also teach you some of the basic skills in dealing with illness and injury.

Learn to listen to what your body is telling you. For most day to day activity your body is simply ticking over. However, once you take up exercise, you are beginning to explore capabilities that you have hardly used before and with which you are unfamiliar. Learn to monitor how you feel and how your body responds so that you recognise abnormalities more quickly. You will come to recognise the healthy soreness in your muscles after a particularly hard workout; you will recognise how your recovery time shortens as you become more fit, so that the unfamiliar pain or unusually fast heart rate will be the early signals that all is not well.

Importance of warm up and preparation

Whilst some injuries are true accidents in the sense of being unavoidable, many are the result of your body being unprepared for tasks that you have set it. If you are unfamiliar with the sport, and lack the techniques and skills involved, it may lead to injury. Fitness is very specific. You may be superbly fit for marathon running, but to enter for a canoeing event without previous training would be to invite the risk of accident or injury.

Warm up is an important part of prevention. You may not be an Olympic athlete but it is just as important for you to spend time on getting the blood circulating through muscles and the stretch back into ligaments that you are about to stress to their limits. Racing drivers do not expect their car engines and tyres to perform at their best until properly warmed up. Neither should you expect your body to perform well when cold. It is a vital part of self-help in preventing injury to spend at least 15-20 minutes warming up and stretching with a routine you have learned.

Lots of injuries happen simply because your body is not prepared for the stresses you are trying to impose. Some of these overuse problems are virtually unavoidable, like the pulled hamstring or calf muscle as you desperately stretch for the 50-50 ball, but others are more predictable. Every sports medicine doctor and physiotherapist knows such problems as the painful kneecaps brought on by the sudden burst of pre-season training after a summer of relaxation and rest. Stress fractures are the response of bones unprepared for a newfound enthusiasm for jogging or a sudden step up in the weekly running mileage in an attempt to catch up on lost training. Your body is capable of achieving almost anything you wish it to do – but you must give it time to adjust and adapt. World records are continually at risk with achievements being made that were thought impossible only a few years ago. Remember, however, that such improvements are the result of months of training, monitored by the increasingly knowledgeable and sophisticated sports scientists.

Self help includes learning about the improvements in training techniques that filter down from the highest levels of sport and which already help to raise standards of performance at all levels.

How to diagnose an injury

When you are injured, the first needs are to try and decide what it is you have done, which will help in the next stage of whether you need to see a doctor, either at once or at the next clinic. In other words, you need a diagnosis. It may not be possible to make a complete diagnosis at once. In many cases, you have to decide what are the likely possibilities and be prepared to adjust your ideas in response to the progress you make.

Like any doctor you have to consider the history, the symptoms and the signs. The history is the story of how the injury happened. It may be the slow onset of increasing soreness or it may be as a result of a specific incident. The symptoms are what you feel. Pain, weakness, breathlessness are all symptoms that help to localise the problem. Signs are those things that you discover by examining the part of the body that is injured. An unusual shape may be due to swelling or to deformity such as a dislocated joint. Tenderness may be very localised over the site of a stress fracture or quite diffuse over an area of bruising. The normal movement of a joint may be limited either by pain or mechanically, as it is when a torn piece of cartilage in the knee joint drifts out of place, jamming the knee movement.

Recognising different kinds of injuries

Muscle injuries are usually a sudden, immediately recognisable event. A direct blow causes immediate pain and may even paralyse the muscle for a few moments so that it refuses to work normally. It may begin to swell up fairly quickly and by the next day is stiff and sore. A muscle pull, where fibres are torn apart from each other, usually happens when it is at the limit of its stretch and you make that extra lunge. Perhaps a sudden burst of activity produces an instant searing pain. Again, it may swell and be stiff and sore on the following day.

The swelling is not always immediately obvious. Being deep down within the body, the associated bleeding may not appear as a bruise and swelling is often diffuse rather than localised. If you are not sure, using a tape measure to compare the injured with the uninjured limb may show quite a difference.

An injured muscle will be painful to use. Passive movement of the joint which the muscle controls may be painfree if the muscle is gently stretched, but as soon as you ask the muscle to do any work it will protest.

Ligaments are those slightly elastic bands of

tissue that hold joints together and limit their movements to within a certain range. Injury to ligaments commonly happen because of a sudden event that overstresses the tissue and it tears. Usually the tear is only partial, but it can be complete and the joint unstable. Swelling is more or less inevitable and bruising may appear after a few hours. There is considerable localised tenderness and gentle stretching of the injured ligament causes pain. All other passive movements of the joint are painless, but it is usually uncomfortable to fully bear weight.

Bone injuries can be the result of direct force, usually a blow or an overwhelming force applied to the bone, but stress fractures are more insidious, being the result of a repeated and regular bending movement. Just as you can eventually break a piece of wire by repeatedly bending it back and forth, so can a hairline fracture occur in bone from the regular bending that is part of its shock absorbing function. The bones of the lower leg bend when running to absorb the shock of heel impact.

There is little doubt when a bone has been broken. The pain is severe and there is considerable local swelling and possibly bruising. Normal movement or weight bearing is more or less impossible. Minor cracks and stress fractures are not nearly so obvious and will probably need special tests such as X-rays or scanning before you can be sure. If there is any doubt, particularly if muscular or ligamentous injury is slow to settle, you should see a doctor.

Injuries to the joint itself, rather than the tissues that surround it, often occur. In a typical moving joint, the opposing bone surfaces are made completely smooth by a covering of softer cartilage and movement is lubricated by oil produced by the lining of the enclosing capsule. The bones are held together by ligaments which are usually outside the capsule and arranged in such a way as to limit movement to a definite range and in definite directions. Opposing groups of muscles control the action of the joint by a delicate balance between those that initiate movement and those which offer resistance. The joint is therefore always stable at any part of its range of movement.

Joints can suffer acute injury as a result of trauma (or a wound) or more chronic problems that develop over a period of weeks, months or even years. Pain is a prominent feature of injury and this will usually affect all movements of the joint. Swelling may be immediate, in which case it is very likely to be due to bleeding within the joint cavity. Since blood is an irritant, it is better removed, particularly from the larger joint, and as it usually denotes serious injury, you should see a doctor as soon as possible. Swelling which develops more slowly after injury is the result of an increased output of lubricating fluid. The need to see a doctor is less urgent but it, too, is usually the result of significant damage and diagnosis may not be easy.

Significance of pain Pain is a symptom and a problem to many sports players. For some, it seems to represent a further challenge, a barrier to be overcome by determination and even harder training. Coaches and athletes alike look on the ability to withstand pain as a virtue. But pain is there for a purpose. It may be a signal that damage has already happened, or a sign that if you continue a particular activity without giving the body chance to recover, something is going to give. Your state of mind has a lot to do with how you appreciate pain and there is no doubt that during the excitement of competition, you are less sensitive to pain than normal.

There is infinite variety to pain. At its lowest intensity, it can be almost pleasurable; the healthy discomfort of muscles that have been exercised hard gives a satisfying feeling of having given your best, but the screaming agony of stiff and sore muscles exercised well beyond the limits for which they are fit is a poweful disincentive for further exercise.

alarm signal, a warning of more serious damage and impending harm.

Children are often said to have growing pains that are brought on by exercise. These can be the result of stressing immature limbs and in no circumstance should they be dismissed as trivial. Osteochondritis is a condition where the growing areas of bones become inflamed and sore as a result of being overstressed. If the stress is continued, damage can result to the bones. Stress fractures are not unusual in the immature bones of children during running or jumping sports. If the pain is ignored, the bone may break completely.

People vary enormously in their capacity to put up with pain. As a general rule, the extrovert, happy-go-lucky type attracted to contact team sports tends to put up with pain rather better than the more introspective anxious type.

Many runners experience pain during competitions as shown here in a gruelling cross-country race uphill through mud. However, class athletes learn to run through the pain and to recognise its source.

Certain events, such as long-distance running and cycle racing, produce pain as a result of the effort involved and if an athlete is to be successful he must develop, through training, a tolerance which allows him to continue despite the discomfort. The art of training is to judge the amount of stress that the body can tolerate when it has still not properly recovered from the previous workout. It is this constant challenge that raises the level of fitness. Too much, too quickly and damage occurs.

If you listen to what your body is telling you, you can quickly learn to differentiate between a pain that comes from a temporary and minor disorder and the pain that is an

Self treatment – RICE

After you have suffered a sports injury, looked at its cause and arrived at a diagnosis, how do you treat it? All sportsmen should memorise the basics of first aid and self treatment after an injury which are summed up in the word RICE – rest, ice, compression and elevation. Not only will doctors and physiotherapists advise this as an initial treatment for even fairly serious injuries but it also is the easiest and most effective form of treatment that the athlete can carry out himself over the 48 hours following an injury.

Rest

It is a well known fact (or maybe it is a myth after all) that the average doctor's reaction to a sports injury is to advise complete rest, stop all sport. Since most sportsmen are terrified of losing fitness this advice is, not surprisingly, usually ignored and training continued, with the real risk of complicating an initially simple injury. In fact, complete rest from all forms of activity is usually unnecessary, but some rest, particularly of the injured part, is essential. Rest is a treatment which needs to be prescribed with the same thought and care as any other and usually some compromise can be reached between the need to promote satisfactory healing without losing too much of that hard-earned fitness. Sportsmen should remember that even if training is stopped altogether, it probably takes as much as two weeks before a significant amount of fitness is lost.

There are a number of conditions that do demand total rest as part of their treatment. The need to rest major fractures is obvious. Most soft tissue injuries should have total rest, together with ice application, for the first 48 hours or so in order to reduce the swelling. A deep bruise of the thigh muscle may progress to a hardened scar if it is exercised too early.

Certain medical conditions also demand rest. Too early a return to training after a virus infection can lead to an inflammation of the heart muscle which may take weeks to settle. If you know your normal resting pulse

Special, elastic air strip bandages help provide protection and support for joints which are most vulnerable to strain – elbows (1), wrists (2), ankles (3) and knees (4). They can be adjusted during play.

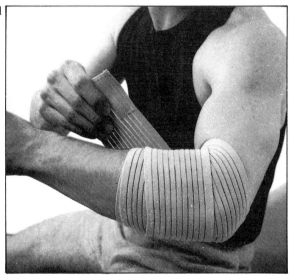

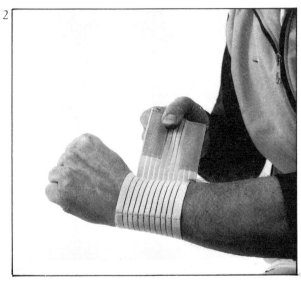

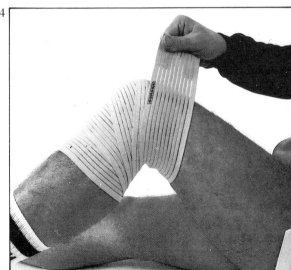

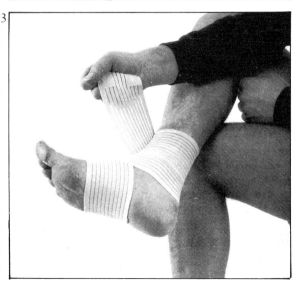

rate, you should wait until it has returned to normal before resuming training after a heavy cold or flu. All individuals have a certain amount of energy available to them each day. An illness demands that a proportion of that energy is used in overcoming it. Trying to sweat off the symptoms by carrying on with training will at best prolong the illness and at worst promote complications.

As we have seen, there are a number of conditions that result from overuse of the body. Stress fractures are usually the result of rhythmic pounding on a hard and unyielding surface. The growth areas of adolescent bones become inflamed when overenthusiastic muscular activity is more than the soft, unformed bony tissue can tolerate. Tenosynovitis is the inflamed tendon sheath resulting from a session of unaccustomed activity, such as the oarsman or canoeist who suddenly increases the amount of intensity of his training or even the DIY enthusiast screwing together his new flat-packed deluxe kitchen.

For these overuse states, a modification of activity is often all that is needed for recovery to take place. Pain is the signal that all is not well. By keeping the activity to below the level of pain, healing will take place. For example, the runner with stress fractures threatening his legs may be able to run a reduced mileage on grass without pain. Certainly there is no reason why he or she should not go through running exercises in the swimming pool, since running while floating in water relieves the skeleton of most of its stresses. Alternatively, if running is painful, cycling may not be.

As recovery takes place, the amount of rest needs to be judged and modified so that return to full activity is progressive.

Ice

The use of ice in the immediate treatment of soft tissue injury is hallowed by tradition even if science is still a little doubtful. Since the body is highly efficient at defending its core temperature, which includes the major muscles, it is arguable that the effect of ice is not particularly deep. What is in no doubt, however, is that thousands of injured sportsmen every year testify to the benefit of cold

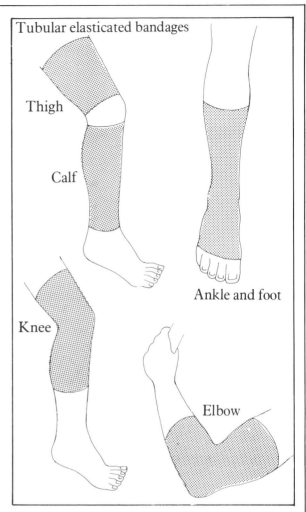

One-piece tubular elasticated bandages can be purchased in most chemists and are specifically designed to support different joints and muscles.

application (whether it be the trainer's magic sponge or the latest in sophisticated instant cold packs), to their bruised and torn muscles and ligaments.

Ice is the most successful of the cold treatments. Ideally, it should be crushed ice, which can be contained in a plastic bag so that the pack can mould itself to the surface of the body and provide a reasonably uniform effect over all the area it covers. The size of the pack should be sufficient to overlap the area being treated by 2.5-5cm (1-2 inches) and because ice burns are a risk, the area should be covered with a thin damp towel over which the ice pack is placed. If no towel is available, substitute a layer of petroleum jelly or similar grease. It is usual to leave the ice pack in place for about 10 minutes and to repeat the treatment every couple of hours during the first 12 hours after injury.

The effect of cold is to restrict the blood supply to the injured area, which, in turn, helps to minimise the swelling that might otherwise restrict the mobility of the injured part. It is important to preserve mobility since that provides the essential stimulus to organised healing.

Cold can be applied in a variety of ways. Best known, but probably least efficient, is the trainer's magic sponge. The cold water just does not remain in contact long enough to do any real good.

Ice from the domestic refrigerator or from an ice-making machine is cheap, widely available and, providing it is crushed, probably provides the most intense cold. It can be easily carried and stored for a reasonable time in a cool bag or cool box. Ready packaged and less likely to leak is the packet of frozen peas. The particle size is about right, the pack size is convenient, it moulds nicely to the contours of the body and it is reusable!

Commercially available ice packs are of two main kinds. The single-use pack which relies on the mixing of two chemicals to produce cold tends to be expensive and probably does not achieve the same levels of cooling as ice. The other variety is the glycerine-filled refreezable pack which is more durable.

More recent is the chemically impregnated foam bandage which relies on evaporation for its cooling effect. Although less cold than ice, it can be completely wrapped around a limb, covering a large area, and in that way may well inhibit the circulation to the acutely injured part. It is reusable, providing it is stored properly after use, and has a useful life of about six hours.

Cold not only cuts down the circulation to the damaged area, restricting the amount of swelling, but it also seems to have a pain-relieving effect. You should always try to ensure that a plentiful ice supply is available wherever sport is taking place. It is safe, unless you produce an ice burn and can only do good to an acute injury.

Compression

Swelling is almost inevitable with any injury and the distension of the tissues not only makes the injury more painful, but also limits the amount of movement possible. The less swelling that occurs and the sooner it is dispersed, the better.

Conventional bandages are effective in discouraging swelling, but the modern tubular elasticated bandages made to suit various limb sizes, are more convenient and easy to use. Used single or double, depending on how firm you need the support to be, they give an even pressure on the limb. Placing a pad over the swollen area and beneath the bandage gives a slightly increased localised pressure. These tubular bandages keep their elasticity reasonably well even after washing, so they can be used several times.

Elasticated and crêpe bandages have to be put on with care, and are not easy to self-apply. It is usual to start at the extremity of a limb and bandage towards the heart. Each turn should overlap the previous one by about half a width of the bandage and should be applied with an even firmness. It is a common mistake to wind them on too tightly, which interferes with the circulation in the limb and can lead to discomfort in fingers and toes. Crêpe bandages in particular lose their elasticity after washing and soon begin to look like pieces of chewed string, when they serve no useful purpose at all.

Elevation

Gravity is a useful aid to reduce swelling and, equally, is a powerful influence in slowing down its disappearance. Almost everyone has experienced the increased pain in a bruised hand or finger if it is left dangling at your side. This is because the congestion in the bruised area is made worse by gravity slowing down the flow of blood from the arm. Almost instinctively, you tend to hold your hand up or rest it up near the opposite shoulder when gravity helps to relieve the congestion.

It helps to elevate a sprained ankle or bruised foot but it is not the slightest bit of use to put it on a low foot stool. If you want gravity to help in draining the swelling, the injury has to be above the horizontal, so it makes more sense to put your feet up on the table or mantlepiece. It may also help to put the foot end of the bed on blocks so that the swelling can more easily disperse overnight.

Recovery period

Administered over the 48 hours following a sports injury, RICE is the most common and effective form of home treatment and when properly adhered to gets the next stage of rehabilitation off to a flying start. Essentially this next stage of recovery involves a programme of increasing activity until you return to normal and will probably include mobility exercises to restore the full range of movement followed by a gradual increase of loading on the tissues to promote healing along the normal lines of stress. For detailed advice on getting back to full function see *Rehabilitation* pages 104-125.

Rehabilitation can be carried out alone or in consultation with your coach or trainer, physiotherapist or doctor. During the recovery period you may need or find helpful other forms of home treatment such as heat and medication.

Heat

Heat is useful to improve the circulation to a healing injury. It is the last thing needed for an acute injury in its early stages, when the aim is to minimise swelling, but, as healing begins to be established, it is helpful to have a good blood supply to the area. For example, stiff muscles that have been too well exercised seem to relax better after a little heat has been applied.

There are all sorts of ways in which heat is applied. Simplest is the hot water bottle, but great care must be taken not to burn the skin and it should always be wrapped in a cloth before being used. Various heat lamps are available, usually using the infrared spectrum. Again, it is possible to burn the skin but their heat is more diffused and does not produce such a localised reaction. The heat is usually applied for about 10 minutes, which will produce a slight reddening and warm feeling in the skin. How much of that heat actually penetrates to the deeper tissues is debatable, as with ice, but it is possible that some kind of chain reaction is set up to encourage an increased blood supply. It is advisable to apply heat no more than two or three times a day to avoid damaging the skin.

Self medication

For some sports players pain is a virtue and pain relievers an admission of failure. Most of us have more sense and appreciate the relief that can be given by a couple of tablets.

For simple relief of pain, paracetamol is the ideal choice. It is readily available in pharmacies and stores under a wide variety of brand names, in both tablet and liquid form. A single tablet is in usually 500mgm strength and the usual adult dose is 1-2 tablets every 4-6 hours. More expensive are the compound preparations which contain, in addition to paracetamol, aspirin and codeine. These compound preparations have no real advantage and codeine is a banned substance in certain sports, so you may therefore fall foul of the doping regulations.

Aspirin is the best known of that group called anti-inflammatory tablets. Most not only relieve pain but also positively act to reduce inflammation and swelling. Given as soon as possible after an injury, they do seem to help minimise the swelling and soreness. Most of the anti-inflammatories other than aspirin are only available on a doctor's prescription, the exception being Ibuprofen, again marketed under a variety of brand names and usually available only in pharmacies and chemist shops. The usual tablet strength is 200mgm and 1 or 2 tablets every 6 hours is the usual dose. However, these tablets can sometimes cause pain or even bleeding in the bowel so that anyone with a history of persistent indigestion should avoid using them or at least ask for medical advice.

Liniments and massage are popular amongst sports players both as a preparation for sport and as a treatment for injury. Most of them contain rubifacient chemicals which inflame the skin slightly, causing redness which both gives a feeling of warmth and acts as a counter-irritant to more deep-seated pain. Some also have added enzymes which are supposed to help the active ingredients penetrate the skin to reach the deeper tissues or help in the early dispersal of bruising.

Since the skin is a very efficient barrier it is unlikely that these various creams and lotions ever achieve much in the way of penetration but they can be comforting, unless you are unfortunate enough to be allergic to them. More benefit is likely to be had from the massage that goes with the application of the creams. Self massage helps before and after the event. Using liniment, lotions or powder as lubrication, firm stroking of the limb towards the heart, rather like pulling on a sock, will help the circulation. This can be alternated with shaking or clapping over the muscles. Massage is initially stimulating, but if it is overdone causes relaxation, so it should be used sparingly before a sports event.

When to seek medical advice

The great majority of injuries that happen in sport are relatively minor and will settle quickly with the measures so far advised. Bruises will usually have settled within a week, although deeper bruises in the larger muscles may take a little longer. Strains and sprains usually take three or four weeks before they are completely better. Although you may be able to walk or even run a little without discomfort a week after spraining your ankle, you will be asking for trouble and a much longer lay-off if you risk it in a sports event. Aches and pains that seem to be the result of overuse should respond to

cutting down your training load and perhaps a change of environment – for example, exercising on grass, or even in the swimming pool, instead of on roads or on the track.

You should look for further advice if you do not progress despite the treatment you have carried out or if the pain of an injury is sufficient to need regular doses of pain-relieving medication. Even the professionals find it difficult to sort out knee problems and if a knee injury or knee pain is not settling after a few days you should seek help. If a particular problem recurs, it may be because of bad technique in your sport or a bio-mechanical problem that needs expert evaluation, so you should think about professional help.

Getting the right medical help

Under normal circumstances, the first person to go to would be your family doctor or family physician. As general practitioners, they have a wide experience of dealing with minor illness and, even if they have no particular knowledge of sports medicine, they can go a long way towards diagnosing your problem and directing you towards the appropriate help if it is needed.

A G.P. can refer to a specialist who will usually be either an orthopaedic surgeon or a consultant in rheumatology or orthopaedic medicine. The surgeon is usually more concerned with trauma or injury to muscles and joints whereas the rheumatologist or orthopaedic physician deals more with inflammation, such as you get with overuse injuries.

If you have a major accident then it's likely that you will go to a casualty or accident and emergency department at a hospital where the immediate problem will be dealt with, after which you will be passed on to the care of an orthopaedic specialist.

Once your problem has been diagnosed by a doctor, either a G.P. or specialist, an important part of your recovery will probably be through treatment from a physiotherapist.

Physiotherapists work both in hospital and in private practice. Those in hospital will normally only accept patients referred by a doctor. Those in private practice will accept patients who refer themselves but if there is any doubt about the problem they will normally require a medical opinion, so it is usually better to see a doctor first. A word of warning: anyone can call himself a physiotherapist, but there are professional qualifications and you should avoid those who are not qualified, however experienced they may claim to be. See *Physiotherapy*, pages 96-103 for further advice on finding a registered physiotherapist.

The feet play a crucial part in contact with the ground and many of those niggling aches and pains in the ankles, knees and legs may be because of a minor defect in the way that they work. These minor abnormalities do not matter until you start hard exercise, when the stresses that result begin to show up. Chiropodists have for a long time looked after corns, warts and blistered feet, but over recent years they have concerned themselves much more with the biomechanics of the feet, including a study of the complexities of their movement called podiatry. If it seems likely that your injury could result from a biomechanical problem your doctor or physiotherapist may suggest a podiatric assessment.

Manipulation is an art that has been sadly neglected by the medical profession but has enthusiastically and skilfully been carried on by chiropracters and osteopaths. Their main success seems to be in relieving spinal aches and pains, but manipulation of other joints can be helpful. These former fringe practitioners are now accepted as responsible professionals who, like physiotherapists, will have completed a proper course of training.

Unfortunately there are a very few places where there is a proper system of sports medicine. Sports injuries clinics do provide this service but those few that exist under the umbrella of a National Health Service are usually very busy and overworked. Increasingly, private clinics are being developed. Usually the costs are modest but, if sport is going to be an important part of your life, you should consider taking out insurance to cover some of the costs of your treatment.

How to deal with common injuries

Cramp

There are many factors that may be responsible for cramp coming on in a muscle during or after exercise. Salt deficiency is rarely the cause and swallowing salt tablets routinely for cramp is not recommended. Tight shoe laces or socks, cold weather and inadequate warm up prior to exercise can all lead to cramp. Dehydration can also cause cramp. It can be prevented by good training with adequate pre-exercise warm up, sensible build-up in training intensity, normal diet with adequate fluids and salt, and correct clothing and footwear. To treat cramp, stop the activity, gently massage and stretch the affected muscle and warm up a cold limb. If cramp is continuous or recurrent, then see a doctor.

Infections

A wound which suggests infection, i.e. increasing pain, swelling, tenderness or redness of the skin, needs to be treated by a doctor. All sportsmen should be actively immunized against tetanus as grass wounds carry with them the risk of tetanus infection. Booster doses of vaccine may be necessary in the case of a dirty wound when immunization is not up to date.

Blisters, scrapes and cuts

In all of these injuries the skin has been damaged, which means that they must be protected and kept as clean as possible. Blisters are an attempt by the body to relieve friction and the fluid acts as a cushion for the tender tissue beneath. There is little point, therefore, in releasing the fluid, which will gradually be reabsorbed by the body. Cover it with a dry dressing and use petroleum jelly to reduce further chafing.

Scrapes or abrasions are common on knees, hips and elbows following a fall on to hard ground. They are often quite extensive and difficult to cover. As far as possible, cover with a clean dressing which can be held in place with adhesive tape or a bandage. These do not last long in the rough and tumble of contact sports, so if a match is in progress probably all you can do is to wash the wound with clean water and apply an antiseptic cream, putting on the dressing later.

Cuts should be covered with a clean dressing after being gently washed with clean warm water. If they are bleeding persistently, press on the dressing with your thumbs or hold up the injured part as high as possible. The edges of a gaping wound can be held together with strips of adhesive tape, although the skin has to be clean and dry if the tape is to stick effectively. Many gaping wounds need to be secured with stitches and this is a job which should be done as soon as possible by a doctor or in a hospital.

A kit for treating blisters is a useful standby for most athletes' kit-bags. This consists of blister padding, protective dressings and adhesive tape.

Strained and bruised muscles

Muscle pulls and strains happen most frequently in the first or last few minutes of a sports event either because the muscle is not warmed up and stretched properly or because of fatigue and the loss of control of overstretching. Bruises generally result from contact with other players or with a hard surface. In both cases the immediate effect is bruising and you should apply the RICE treatment, following by gentle but progressive rehabilitation.

Sprained joints

Bleeding is almost inevitable along with considerable swelling so the immediate need is for rest, ice and elevation. After 48 hours, you should start to move the joint gently through as full a range of movement as possible and, as healing progresses, start to gradually increase the load on the joint as you work it. Rehabilitation is not complete until you have tested the joint under full load. The

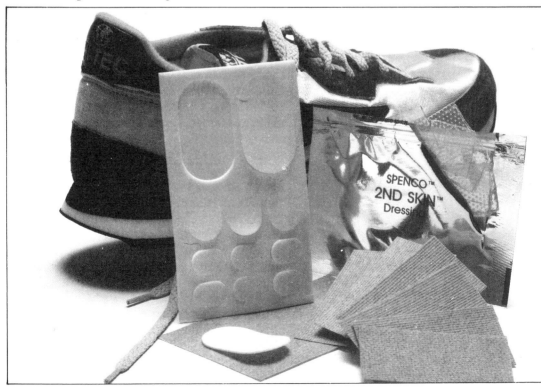

commonest sprain is of an ankle joint; the following simple exercises are graduated to encourage a sensible rehabilitation and can be easily done at home.

Exercises for ankle sprain

1 After the first two days, start to gently rotate the joint through its full range of movement about ten times every hour.

2 After a further couple of days, add the following exercise to the mobility exercises. While sitting in a chair and with your foot on the ground, rock the foot backwards and forwards. Lift the heel off the floor, then rock the foot back onto the heel and lift the toes off the floor. Next, still in the same position, rock the foot from side to side – first to the outside edge, then to the inside edge.

3 When the ankle begins to feel stronger, try the exercises while standing evenly balanced on each foot. Support yourself, if necessary, and rise up onto your toes, then rock back onto your heels. Alternatively, stand on the edge of a stair and alternately rise onto your toes and then let your heels drop below the level of the stair. While sitting with crossed ankles, press the outer borders of your feet together for a count of five and relax. Repeat all these exercises in groups of 10, three or four times a day.

4 As improvement continues, start to walk longer distances and begin to re-educate the important sensors in your ankle that control balance. Stand on the injured leg with your eyes closed and balance for as long as possible several times a day.

5 Gentle jogging is the next step, slowly, for short distances and on grass. Increase the amount of jogging as you feel comfortable, introducing a weaving pattern from time to time to encourage the sense of balance.

6 Some 3 to 4 weeks after the injury when the ankle is stronger, you should be able to run comfortably on harder surfaces such as road or track and be able to make sudden stops or changes of direction without pain. Shuttle runs are a good test, running hard backwards and forwards between two points.

Knee pain

Knee injuries are often difficult to sort out and to treat and you would be well advised to seek help from a doctor rather than attempt home treatment. One knee problem that does respond well to self-help, however, is the pain around the kneecap caused by overuse. Because of insufficient muscle development, the underside of the kneecap becomes inflamed due to misalignment during exercise of the knee. As a general rule, the pain is increasingly worse on exercise, particularly when going up or down stairs or hills.

If dealt with in its early stages, it settles readily. First of all, rest by reducing activity to below the pain level or by trying a different exercise that does not cause pain. Each day, with the affected leg held straight and the foot at right angles to the leg, do 100 straight leg raises, splitting the exercise up into two or three sessions. As the exercise becomes easier, add resistance by weighting the foot, perhaps with a pillow. If there is no improvement in a week, seek medical advice.

Shin splints

Pain on the front of the leg coming on after exercise, often taking longer and longer to disappear at rest, may be due to the muscle swelling that always occurs with exercise distending the fairly rigid compartment in which it is contained. If you ignore it, it will progress and could become chronic.

It is an overuse condition. Ice is the immediate treatment with complete rest and elevation for a few days to let the congestion settle down. When you start back to activity, begin at a lower level and increase gradually to allow your body to adapt. If the condition fails to settle, it may be that the pain is the result of a stress fracture and you should seek medical help.

Self-help comes from self knowledge. Most sports carry with them a risk of injury, usually minor and easily dealt with. If they are not managed properly in the early stages they can become major problems. A lot of opportunity exists to learn more about treatment; in the columns of sports magazines, through courses run by sports governing bodies or sport medicine associations. Courses cost very little and the investment is amply repaid if you can help yourself recover more quickly from injury.

First-aid kit

The sports player's first-aid kit is an essential standby for self-help. Treating an injury immediately after it has happened can save days in the recovery period. It is important that you remember to replace, straight away, items that you or colleagues have used. The kit need not be expensive, but it is false economy to try and make things last forever. Tablets become out of date, crêpe and elastic bandages lose their stretchiness and unused pieces from sterile packs become contaminated. Replace not only what you have used, but check regularly for outworn or outdated items.

Scissors Blunt-ended or bandage scissors, with a flattened end to one blade, avoid skin damage when cutting off bandages or strapping.

Nail clippers Stout nail clippers may be better than scissors to trim an overgrown or damaged nail.

Safety pins In various sizes, these are always useful for a number of purposes, apart from securing dressings or bandages.

Needle A blunt needle, the tip of which has been heated in the flame of a match, can be used to gently bore a hole to release the very painful bruises that can occur beneath a finger or toenail. Do not be put off by the smell of singed nail.

Bandages *Tubular elastic bandages* can be bought in a variety of sizes to suit both arms and legs. They are easily put on to hold dressings in place and, applied as a double layer, are effective in discouraging swelling. A useful length is 1 metre (3.6 feet). Remember that they do age, so replace them after they have been used a few times. *Crêpe bandages* are used in the same way, but they tend not to stay in place as well and they age more quickly.

Zinc oxide strapping This non-stretch strapping, in a roll 2.5cms (1 inch) wide, is useful for securing dressings and bandages and to strap injured small joints.

Dressings *Elastic fabric dressing strips* can be bought either individually wrapped in a variety of sizes or as a continuous length from which the right-sized strip is cut. *Gauze swabs* and non-adherent dressings can be bought in individual sterile packs, the most useful size being 10 x 10cms (4 x 4 inches). *Adhesive strips* to pull the edges of a gaping wound together are a useful addition to the first-aid kit. Do make sure that the skin surface is clean and dry, otherwise they will not stick. Cover the closed wound with a dry dressing.

Disinfectant Warm water is sufficient to clean wounds before dressing them, but you can add a small amount of disinfectant if you wish.

Orthopaedic felt or foam This adhesive-backed padding can be used to protect a chafed or sore area by cutting it into a ring or a U-shaped dressing. A heel pad will help in treating a sore Achilles tendon, and appropriately placed and shaped pads beneath a pressure bandage will help to discourage swelling after injury.

Ice It is not always practicable to carry ice or prefrozen packs around with you. Instant cold packs, which rely on the mixing of two chemicals, are not cheap but are better than nothing. The cooling bandage, which is a fairly recent product, is perhaps best for convenience and effectiveness.

Petroleum jelly This is useful as a preventative measure on those areas, such as the inside of the thighs, which become sore from chafing. A Vaseline smeared gauze pad may prevent chafing in vulnerable areas beneath a supportive strapping.

Medication *Paracetamol* is the most suitable pain reliever. Anti-inflammatory tablets, such as *Ibuprofen*, may lessen the effects of a soft tissue injury if they are used straight away. *Anti-fungal powders*, available in a wide range of packs, are effective in both prevention and treatment of athlete's foot and similar infections. Some people however, develop an allergic reaction to them.

A well-equipped first-aid kit is a 'must' for every sportsman and sportswoman. At most races and competitions there is first-aid expertise on hand in case of injuries, as shown here in the treatment of a pulled hamstring.

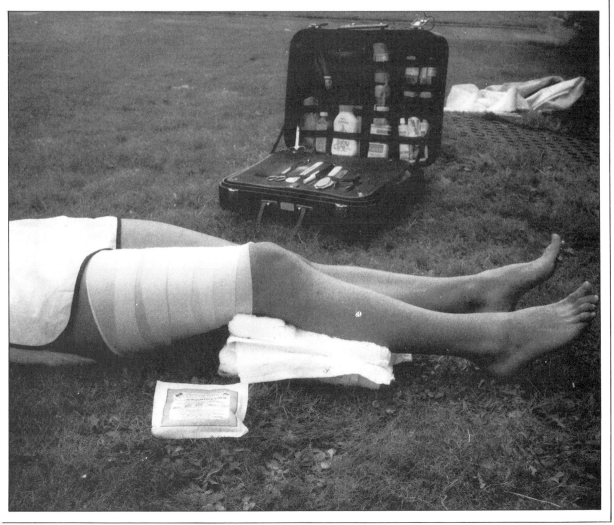

PHYSIOTHERAPY

Ideally, the physiotherapist should be involved in both prevention and treatment of sports injury but, in practice, he or she is most often consulted some time after the injury has occurred, usually because pain or discomfort has persisted. One obvious exception to this is the professional sports club which employs its own physiotherapist who is actively involved in fitness training for the sport in question and who gives individual therapy or specific treatment and exercise programmes to club players as and when necessary. Physiotherapists should, in fact, be used by all serious sports people to help them train properly for their chosen sport, not merely consulted after an injury has occurred – which could, perhaps, with their help, have been prevented in the first place. Many health clubs now have consultant physiotherapists on their staff and sports enthusiasts are well advised to seek their help *before* taking up a new sport or returning to a familiar one after a lapse of time. Assuming, however, that you have sustained a sports injury and you have been advised to see a physiotherapist, where do you find one?

Finding a physiotherapist

First of all, in most cases you need to be referred to a physiotherapist by your doctor and it is important that you find a qualified physiotherapist. In Great Britain, a Chartered Physiotherapist is one who has had a three or four year training at a school recognised by the Chartered Society of Physiotherapy. This is the only training in Britain accepted for state registration and one has to be state registered to work in the National Health Service. Chartered Physiotherapists work in NHS hospitals, private practice, private hospitals, health centres, industry and in sports clubs.

You can normally only be seen in the casualty department of an NHS hospital on the day of injury or the day after, if your injury is considered an emergency. Consultants in out-patients clinics usually have long waiting lists and do require a referral from your own doctor. A few NHS hospitals have sports clinics, so ring up and enquire.

There are many physiotherapists in private practice and they are usually interested in sports injuries. Your doctor may be able to recommend one in your area. Alternatively, contact the Association of Chartered Physiotherapists in Sports Medicine (see page 000) which has 500 members who are specifically interested in sports injuries. Charges are quite reasonable and there are also medical insurance schemes that help pay physiotherapy fees. Your local physiotherapist will give you details.

Many private hospitals are now opening sports clinics as a commercial proposition. You can generally be seen with a minimum of formality and some are even open at weekends. Charges are usually on a time basis whicn works out more expensive than consulting a private practitioner. Insurance is a help, if you remember to get insured before you get injured.

Health centres in the community and at

colleges and universities often employ the services of a physiotherapist. Ask your doctor. Some large companies employ their own physiotherapist and this, of course, overcomes the problem of taking time off work. Your personnel officer should be able to advise. Also, physiotherapists working for professional clubs will sometimes treat local sportsmen and many amateur clubs have the services of a physiotherapist, who attends on training night and match days to deal with any injury problems. It is worth making enquiries if there are such clubs in your locality.

Types of physiotherapy treatment

The physiotherapist is skilled in the use of many forms of physical treatment which can be used to help the injured sportsman. The choice will depend on the nature of the injury, the stage of recovery, what is available at the time and the physiotherapist's choice of treatment based on experience. Ice treatments are commonly used by physiotherapists not only as a first-aid treatment but also later, as are various forms of heat treatment and exercise.

Ice is the most effective, commonly available substance that can be used in the treatment of most sports injuries. It is generally accepted as an important part of first-aid and self-help treatment (see Self help, page 82) and can also be used for further treatment.

The immediate effects of ice are the relief of pain, decrease of muscle spasm and decrease in blood flow. These are followed by increase in blood flow, reduction of swelling and the promotion of healing.

How ice treatment works

When an ice pack is applied to an injury, the brain becomes more aware of the sensation of cold than the pain of injury. This is known as

The physiotherapist's first task is to assess the injury by determining its nature and seriousness, since this affects the type of treatment recommended.

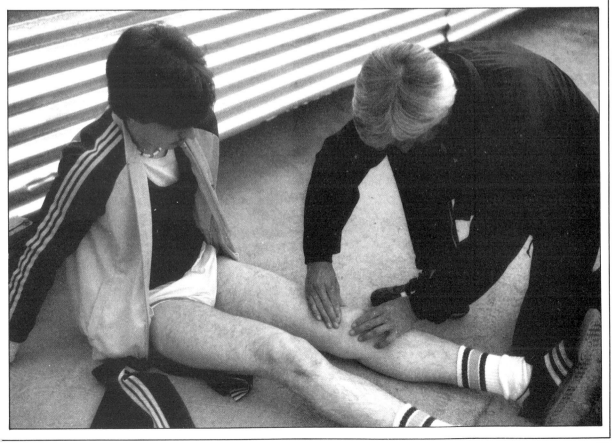

the counter-irritant effect. As the injured part gets colder, the sensitivity of pain nerve endings is reduced and pain impulses are transmitted more slowly. The area becomes anaesthetised or numb. In this anaesthetised state, it would be unwise to resume vigorous activity for fear of doing further damage. When the body is injured, muscles around the injury become very tense. This increased tension produces more pain. This is known as the pain-spasm-pain cycle. Ice reduces pain and the stretch reflex and so allows the muscles to relax and break up the cycle. The blood circulation's response to ice is, first of all, for the vessels near the surface to constrict in order to limit heat loss. This reduces blood flow and slows down the development of swelling. Yet because continued ice treatment beyond 15 to 20 minutes threatens the health of the tissues, a natural reflex expansion of the blood vessels follows. This increases the blood flow in the area, washes away waste products and brings in the body's repair materials. Coupled with this, blood vessel walls expand, becoming more permeable and facilitating the passage of materials.

As a first-aid measure, a brief application of ice should generally be used (10 to 15 minutes) with the aim of limiting blood flow and swelling. When used for treatment at a later stage, the ice is left on for 20 to 30 minutes to increase circulation.

How ice is applied

Ice packs Most physiotherapy departments have ice machines that produce flaked ice. A small towel is soaked in cold water and wrung out. A few handfuls of ice are placed in the middle of the towel and the sides folded over. The pack is placed on the injured part and the couch protected with waterproof sheets and towels. If only cube ice is available, this should be broken up so that it moulds to the injured part. Fair-skinned people may need to protect the skin with olive oil if ice packs are to be applied frequently.

Ice massage Small areas can be massaged with an ice cube or an ice cone made in a polystyrene cup.

Ice soaks Swollen hands or feet can be soaked in a bowl containing water and flaked ice. If the injured part becomes too uncomfortable, expose it to the air for a minute and then put back in the iced water.

Alternative forms of cold

Cold sprays Aerosol sprays containing ethylchloride, chloromethane or fluoromethane are useful as a first-aid measure. However, their effects are superficial and temporary and they should be used exactly as the manufacturer instructs, as they can cause frostbite.

Flexible gel packs These can be cooled in the freezer box of a fridge and taken to the sports venue in an insulated picnic box containing some ice. The gel pack can be used several times before it becomes too warm to be effective and in an emergency, the ice in the insulating box can also be used.

Chemical cold packs These contain a sachet of one chemical surrounded by a second chemical. When the sachet is burst by a firm blow, the two chemicals mix and produce an instant cold pack. These are useful for a physiotherapist travelling with a team when the availability of ice is uncertain. However, chemical cold packs have their limitations. They are not as cold as ice packs and soon warm up and, although useful for first aid, they are not for prolonged treatment. Most types can only be used once.

Contrast bathing This form of treatment combines the benefits of heat and cold. It is useful for hands, wrists, feet and ankles. The injured part is soaked in cold water (50° to 60°F) for one minute, then soaked in hot water (100° to 110°F) for about three minutes and the procedure repeated 4 - 5 times. This is a very effective method of reducing swelling.

Ice should never be placed directly on the skin but wrapped in a small towel or something similar.

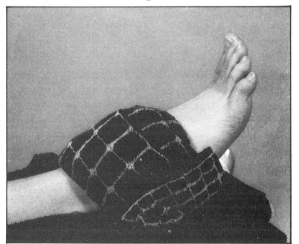

An ice pack, wrapped in a towel to protect the skin from ice burns, will remain cold for about 40 minutes.

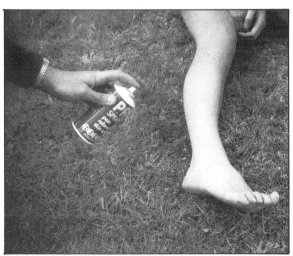

Cold sprays, which do not penetrate deeply, are useful for treating shins and ankles where skin is close to the bone.

Dangers of cold treatments

Although easy to apply and generally effective, cold treatments do have their risks. Because the skin temperature is lowered, the health of the tissues can be damaged. To minimise this, always make sure there is a layer of towel between the ice and the skin – and prolonged application of ice packs beyond 30 minutes is not recommended. In ice massage, the ice should be kept moving all the time.

Patients with poor circulation in their toes or fingers should never be given cold soaks and, needless to say, if any patient experiences extreme discomfort during one or other of the forms of cold treatment, the treatment should stop immediately.

Ultrasound

Ultrasound is a form of heat and massage treatment in which high-frequency sound energy is produced by passing an alternating current through a quartz or quartz substitute crystal. The physiotherapist either applies a 'coupling medium' in the form of a gel (produced by the machine's manufacturer) to the injured part or treats the injured area in water.

How ultrasound works

The sound energy passes through the skin and causes the body tissue to vibrate at its own frequency. This minute vibration acts like a micro-massage with the depth of penetration depending on the frequency. One million cycles per second (1MHz), for example, will penetrate more deeply than three million cycles (3MHz).

The beam of ultrasound can be produced continuously or it can be pulsed. The continuous beam produces a considerable amount of heat in the tissues while the pulsed beam, although producing little heat, still has the micro-massaging effect. Generally, the pulsed beam is used near bony surfaces to avoid possible damage to tissue through over-heating. Usually, ultrasound is not given on the day of the injury because it can cause more bleeding within the tissues, although some physiotherapists believe that the 3MHz beam on low intensity is gentle enough not to cause tissue damage; some may therefore advise treating the injured part almost at once. As a general rule, low intensities are given to recent injuries and higher to more long-standing injuries. Treatment usually starts at 2-3 minutes for recent injuries and increases to 5-6 minutes. Ultrasound should be quite painless and any patient who feels pain or discomfort should immediately inform the physiotherapist; it can simply mean that the intensity is too high.

Effects of ultrasound

The heat and micro-massage produced by ultrasound relieve pain because of their effect on sensory nerve endings. This causes smooth muscles surrounding blood vessels to relax and so improves local circulation and

Ultrasound is frequently used to relieve the pain of hamstring strain and helps soften scar tissue, thereby making stretching easier.

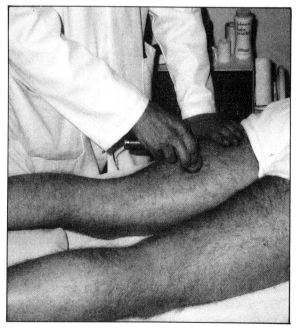

helps the healing process. Ultrasound also has a softening effect on scar tissue and adhesions and therefore makes stretching easier.

Dangers of ultrasound

There are few dangers other than burning but with the correct technique this should never happen. Because the techniques are quite complicated, ultrasound should only be administered by a qualified physiotherapist.

Heat treatment

There are various types of heat treatment usually administered by a physiotherapist some 48 hours after the sports injury has occurred. Remember that heat should not be used as a first-aid treatment because the increase in circulation could lead to more swelling and internal bleeding. Heat treatments can be either deep or superficial, depending on the nature of the injury. Among deep heat treatments are short wave diathermy, microwave and continuous ultrasound. Superficial treatments include infra red, heating pads, hot packs and hot socks.

How heat treatment works

Heat affects the body by increasing circulation and metabolism and by decreasing muscle spasm and pain. It is interpreted by the brain as a pleasant sensation, provided it is not too hot, and has a soothing effect on sensory nerve endings. The smooth muscle surrounding blood vessels relaxes and the vessels expand bringing more blood to the area which, in turn, helps wash away waste products and substances released by damaged tissue.

Heat also increases metabolic rate and as a natural sequence the repair processes in the body are stimulated. As waste products are washed away and the body appreciates the feeling of warmth, tense muscles will relax and pain is reduced.

Shortwave diathermy is a deep-heat treatment which uses a rapidly alternating current to produce heating throughout the injured part. The only sensation of heat is on the skin and the patient should experience a pleasant warmth.

Microwave produces deep heat by using a special valve called a magnetron. Energy is transferred by a reflector placed about 7.5 cm (3 inches) from the skin, and heat penetrates to about 5 cm (2 inches), or slightly less than short wave.

Infrared lamps apply heat to the skin surface and can be useful to relieve stiffness or to treat certain superficial injuries. Small infrared lamps are available for home use and can be bought in many stores.

Electric heat pads are like small electric blankets which are applied to the injured area. Although the heat is superficial, they are very comforting and can be beneficial in easing stiffness associated with back and neck injuries.

Dangers of heat treatment

With all heat treatments, the danger is burning. To avoid this, skin should be dry before treatment begins and should be tested for normal responses to heat and cold – sensation could be lacking where tissue is scarred. Remember that heat treatments should always feel comfortably warm, *not* hot, and if a patient feels pain or discomfort it is essential to inform the physiotherapist.

Recent developments

These include machines which produce energy or stimulation but without the risk of heat.

Pulsed electro magnetic energy (PEME) is a development from short-wave diathermy in which energy is broken up into short pulses. Although this means that no heat is actually produced, more energy can be driven into the body tissues without risk, thereby helping to relieve pain and stimulating healing, too. It is also thought that PEME can help to repair some cell damage. Treatment time depends on the size of the unit used. On the large models, which are found in many clinics and hospitals, this is usually about 10-15 minutes; on the lower-output portable models, which are often taken to sports clubs or on tour, the treatment time is longer.

Laser is now widely used in medicine, from the power laser used by the surgeon, the soft laser by the skin specialist to the mid laser used by physiotherapists. The laser beam penetrates the skin but produces very little heat and is absorbed in the tissues to a depth of just over 2.5 cm (one inch). Its most immediate effect is the relief of pain but it is also said to stimulate healing.

Tens (Transcutaneous electrical nerve stimulation) involves a weak electric current applied to the patient by two electrodes taped to the skin. The main purpose of TENS is to relieve pain and by experimenting with the frequency and pulse width, the patient is usually able to find a combination which produces a tingling sensation and almost immediate pain relief. TENS units are generally available and can be used for self help. However, bear in mind that it is unwise to use TENS for recent injuries while still carrying on normal training, since it could break down new tissue and take the injury longer to heal. TENS is, it seems, most useful for treating old injuries where healing is nearly complete but pain is still present.

Electro-acupuncture probes are incorporated in some TENS units which pick up changes in electrical resistance over acupuncture points and the site injury. Treatment of these points with short duration pulses has proved beneficial to many patients, although how acupuncture works has not yet been fully explained.

Interferential treatment consists of two medium-frequency currents which 'interfere' (interact) to produce a low-frequency current (from 1-200Hz) which passes through the skin easily and is known to be beneficial to circulation, pain and muscle contractions. The frequency can be varied to achieve different effects. At around 100 Hz, for example, the patient will experience considerable pain relief. A rhythmical swing from 1-100Hz, on the other hand, will have a marked effect on circulation while low frequencies will cause strong muscle contractions – which, in turn, have a pumping effect on circulation and help reduce swelling.

Mobilisations and manipulations

To a physiotherapist, mobilisations are the specialised techniques for restoring the full, painless range of movement in joints. The system was made popular by Geoff Maitland in Australia and is very detailed, although the theory is quite simple. Every joint should have a full pain-free range of movement and should withstand overpressure at the limit of the range without pain. If not, then something is wrong and must be put right. Maitland describes the technique as the gentle coaxing of a movement by passive, rhythmical oscillations performed within or at the limit of range. The techniques can be modfied to produce mainly pain relief or mainly increase the range of movement.

Manipulation is performed when a joint is taken to the end of its existing but limited range (because of injury) and a short sharp thrust applied to produce more movement. Manipulations are performed to break down adhesions that are preventing the full range of movement, to free a 'locked joint' or to reposition damaged disc material. Manipulations are not without their dangers and should only be performed by physiotherapists trained in the technique.

Massage

The profession of physiotherapy developed from massage but nowadays few physiotherapists use massage in their everyday work although it is still valuable in the treatment of most sports injuries. When carried out by a physiotherapist or trained masseur, it helps get rid of waste products and increases blood flow. When done slowly and rhythmically, it aids relaxation and, when done briskly, it has a stimulating effect.

Massage techniques

Effleurage is a stroking movement, in which even pressure is applied throughout. It is always done in the direction of the return circulation and is useful for the relief of swelling and tension.

Kneading is a circular motion with alternate pressure and relaxation, the pressure always towards the heart. Both techniques are usually done with the flat hand moulded to the injured part but kneading can be done to small areas with the ends of the fingers or thumbs.

Frictions are a specialized form of massage in which the physiotherapist places a finger directly on the injured tissue and applies pressure to and fro across the line of fibres. The aim is to prevent or stretch out adhesions and, although a little pain is felt at first, the injured area soon becomes anaesthetised.

Exercise

Exercise is an important part of almost every physiotherapy treatment but especially so in the case of sports injuries when as rapid a return as possible to sporting activity is always desirable.

Don't strain, be guided by pain

Physiotherapists would naturally like to see all injuries within a day or two of their occurrence but many sportsmen do not seek treatment for several days or even weeks. In nearly all injuries, the affected part cannot be used normally and even after a few days there will be a noticeable wastage of muscle – for example, in the thigh after a knee injury – if no exercise is done. There may also be a considerable loss of strength and mobility. Compared to normal training, the first exercises introduced by the physiotherapist will seem very tame but this is because healing tissue can be very easily broken down. Free exercise is often given first and the rule is 'a little and often.'

Types of exercise

In the case of, say, a knee injury, the physiotherapist will probably use isometric contractions – where the muscle is contracted as hard as pain will allow without producing movement. The contraction is held for six seconds and then repeated about six times.

After a few days resistance is introduced, generally using weights, weight and pulley circuits or manual resistance from the physiotherapist. This will be the maximum that the patient can overcome without pain and usually bears no relationship to the resistance that the sportsman can normally overcome.

Movement, at first limited by pain and then because connective tissue in muscle or around joints has shortened, is never forced. The physiotherapist will advise the patient to achieve this gradually by moving slowly to a comfortable limit and staying there. As this gets easier, the patient moves a little further, stays there and repeats the exercise, gradually extending his mobility a little at a time.

Maintaining fitness

With any sports injury, overall fitness can quickly be lost and in order to prevent this the physiotherapist tries to work the patient as hard as possible without putting the injury at risk. A lower limb injury, for example, may prevent running but not swimming or cycling; an upper limb injury may prevent swimming but not running or general exercise.

The stationary bicycle and the rowing machine are particularly useful for maintaining fitness and a simple circuit could be:

- Stationary bicycle – 1 minute
- Press-ups – near maximum
- Rowing machine – 1 minute
- Bent knee sit-ups – near maximum
- Step-ups on small stool – 1 minute
- Face down, back extensions – near maximum

The circuit could be repeated two or three times and, in consultation with the physiotherapist, the patient could add favourite exercises, providing they do not cause pain to the injury. As always, the rule is 'Don't strain, be guided by pain'.

Testing fitness

Ideally, the patient should continue physiotherapy treatment until he is totally fit and can return to full training. Too many sportsmen, however, are impatient and give up too soon, only to find that they are not fully recovered. This really is foolish and every sportsman should stay with their physiotherapist until they pass a thorough fitness test.

The physiotherapist plans this carefully, looking especially for signs that the injury may not be fully recovered. The test starts in the treatment room when the injured part is put through the full range of movement and made to work against strong resistance. There should be no pain and power should be almost normal. The patient is then taken to a gym or open space and asked to do vigorous exercise such as running forwards, backwards and sideways. Finally, the patient is taken through the motions of his or her particular sport. If at any stage there are signs of pain, the test should obviously be stopped. This, however, happens rarely when treatment has been carefully carried out.

REHABILITATION

The main consideration in the rehabilitation of an injured person is to return him or her to complete functional fitness in the shortest possible time. For the average patient, rehabilitation is finished when they can walk without a limp, climb stairs and return to work. However, for sports people it must progress to a greater degree in order to cope with the demands of the sport. Therefore, when planning a rehabilitation programme, the goal is to return sports people back to a level of fitness so that they can undertake full training without any limitations. For professional footballers at a rehabilitation centre, this is when they are able to return to full club training – and it is the physiotherapist's task to make sure they can take part in coaching activities without worries. Rehabilitation should commence from the moment the injury occurs. Even though the patient may be limited by pain, swelling and loss of movement in the affected part, it is important that the rest of the body is not forgotten and that the unaffected limbs and cardiovascular system are exercised to maintain as high a level of fitness as possible within the limitations of the injury.

Ideally, rehabilitation should be carried out under the supervision of a physiotherapist and preferably at a sports rehabilitation centre. Even if this is not possible, the aims of rehabilitation are the same for both amateur and professional sportsmen. In planning a rehabilitation programme, these factors must be considered: the injury itself, the injured sportsman's general fitness and the requirements of the particular sport.

Protecting the injury

When planning any programme, it is most important that the injury is not provoked in any way. Therefore, make sure that no activities are introduced too early that may exacerbate the original injury. When rehabilitating ankle or knee injuries, for example, it is pointless for the patient to run before he or she can comfortably walk without a limp. If this is done, not only may the original injury be irritated, but the whole mechanics of the activity could be altered and injury caused in other areas. Remember that in rehabilitating an injured limb, the aim is to regain range of movement, increase strength and re-educate coordination but without causing further injury or exacerbation of the original one.

Maintaining fitness

General fitness of the cardiovascular system and the unaffected limbs can be maintained very soon after the injury has occurred, even though the affected limb may be immobilised. If these areas are neglected until the injured part has recovered, then the whole process of rehabilitation will take much longer because the general level of fitness has dropped. It is therefore essential that exercise programmes are planned to maintain this area of fitness – for example, using a static bicycle even though one leg is encased in plaster. If the non-injured leg cycles with the foot strapped to the pedal and the injured limb is rested with the foot on a stool clear of the bicycle, then cardiovascular fitness can be maintained. Therefore, the second main aim in rehabilitation is to maintain and increase the general fitness of the sportsman, no matter what limitations are imposed by the injury. Once the injured part has returned to a pain-free, functional level then the whole fitness programme can be increased in order to help the sportsman regain specific fitness for his particular sport.

A static bicycle can be used to maintain fitness, even when one leg is immobilised through injury.

Requirements of the particular sport

The final considerations are the requirements of the person's sport which more often than not demands 'fitness' of a specific kind. It is, therefore, of great value if the therapists concerned with rehabilitation of sports people have a knowledge of the particular sports in which they are dealing since this will enable them to understand the demands and rigours that are likely to be put on the sportsman. It is not necessary for the therapist to have played the sport to any great level, but a basic knowledge of the three R's (rules, rigours and rewards) certainly helps. Because of their injury, many sportsmen are not only depressed, but also frightened, particularly if they are professional players. It is, therefore, imperative that the physiotherapist is sympathetic but firm and wherever possible explains the reasons for particular exercises. This helps the injured person to understand their relevance rather than seeing them as a series of unrelated exercises. Also, wherever possible the skills of the sport should be adapted to the exercise programmes, but of course, without endangering the injury.

Before discussing any programmes or exercise regimes, there are certain considerations that have to be mentioned, all of which have an important part to play when planning rehabilitation.

Running in rehabilitation programme

There is a fallacy that one needs to run to get fit, when in fact, one needs to be fit to run! Too often, patients are pushed into running too early or do so themselves as a self-help measure, which not only exacerbates previous injuries but also causes problems in other areas. General cardiovascular fitness can be increased by other activities such as cycling and swimming, as well as running. Therefore, running should be one of the last activities introduced and then only when the sportsman is able to walk without any marked alteration in his gait. At most rehabilitation centres, running is not introduced until the final phase, when the patients are able to walk 2-3 miles without any discomfort in the injured part. However, at this stage, the general fitness is usually high because the preceding programmes have included a lot of cycling, swimming and general fitness circuit training – and the ability to run is one of the final targets to aim at. The specific skills for the sports then become an easy extension of this activity.

Equipment

It is not necessary to have a vast array of technical or specialised equipment in order to plan and execute effective rehabilitation programmes. Obviously, the more equipment that is available, then the more variety of regimes that can be introduced. However, it is possible to plan an hour's strenuous exercise using one blanket only. All that is required is a little forethought and motivation. There is also a danger that with too much equipment, too many exercises will be given and the effectiveness may be lost. Therefore, it is often more beneficial to perform a few exercises correctly and effectively rather than many exercises using a lot of equipment.

Rehabilitation time

In a full-time rehabilitation centre, patients undergo 'treatment' all day, every day so that in an average week they will spend 30 hours in treatments of various kinds. However, because of work, school or other commitments, many injured sportsmen cannot have concentrated treatment of this kind. Therefore, if an injury would require one week's concentrated treatment in a rehabilitation centre – but can only be treated for one hour per day – then obviously the length of time

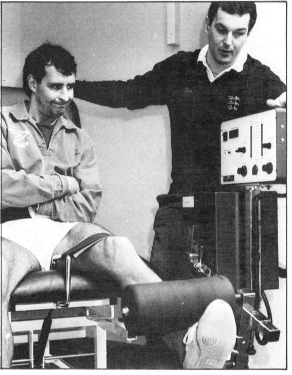

An isokinetic machine, available in only some sports centres, strengthens muscles through resistance.

for recovery is going to be much longer. It is, very important that the injured person is aware of the need to spend time in carrying out treatment programmes. If only one hour, three times a week can be spent on rehabilitation, then an injury that requires 30 hours full-time treatment is going to take up to 10 weeks to be fully healed. Patients who have to follow this type of rehabilitation must be aware of this and take responsibility themselves for carrying out a full programme. If simple effective programmes are given, then the 'little and often' maxim should work well. Clearly, the more time spent in undertaking correct exercise programmes will make for a quicker recovery and better general fitness.

Rehabilitation treatment

Too often, the word 'treatment' is misinterpreted by injured sportsmen, especially when treatment is being carried out at a

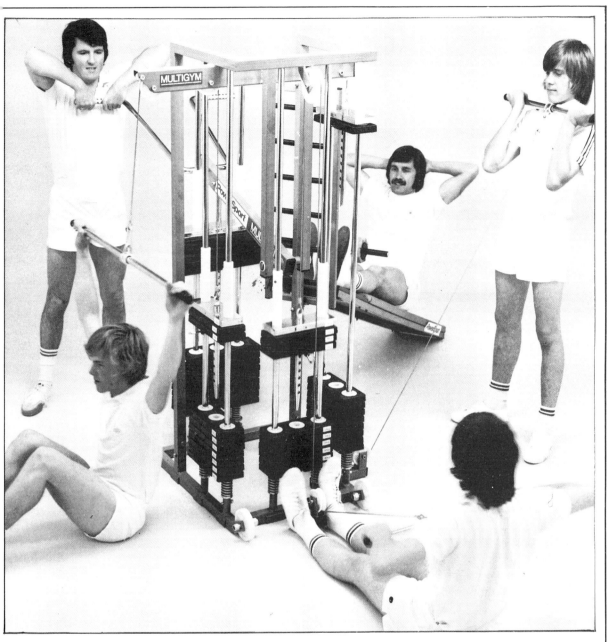

rehabilitation centre. It is frequently felt that treatment only takes place while the patient is actually on a treatment couch. In a rehabilitation centre, treatment begins from the moment the injured person enters the centre until the time he or she is discharged. Warm ups, exercises, cycling, swimming and psychological counselling are all important parts of the 'treatment' package, as well as what is done on the individual plinths. This is something that patients must be aware of at an early stage, otherwise they will not have the right approach to all the exercises and other activities undergone.

Fixed light weights, as in this multi-gym, can be used to increase the resistance of injured limbs in the latter stages of rehabilitation.

Individual attention is only one part of the whole programme and the patient who expects it all of the time is likely to be frustrated and unresponsive to the other very necessary aspects of treatment.

Holistic approach

Both the therapist and the injured person

should understand that treatment must be holistic – that is, it involves the whole person. Too often, much time is wasted concentrating on the injured limb and the rest of the body is neglected. Although it is important to treat the injury, it is as important to remember that the patient is a whole being and not just an ankle, knee, elbow, etc. It is, therefore, essential to exercise all the unaffected parts, provided the exercises do not endanger the recovery of the injured limb. It is also important that besides physical treatment, the patient has psychological support, encouragement, guidance and at all times guarded optimism from the therapist or sports colleagues.

Weights in rehabilitation and training

There is much controversy surrounding the use of weights in rehabilitation and training and the subject is likely to provoke discussions and arguments between coaches from all sports, each of whom will have different ideas and thought about their use. In rehabilitation, lightweights should only be used to increase the resistance in the latter stages of strengthening injured limbs. Heavyweights should not be used, as they will often affect the mechanics of general movement in such a way that joints may be easily injured. However, once full range of joint movement has been regained and the sportsman can safely support his body weight, then the introduction of lightweights with high repetition will help increase the strength of the injured and non-injured limbs. Either free-standing weights, such as dumb bells and weight boots, or fixed weights, as in modern multi-gym equipment, can be used. Bodyweight is a useful alternative to free-standing weights and a series of exercises can be devised to be used at home without supervision. Finally, there is now the added advantage of *isokinetics* which is a relatively new concept in dynamic exercise. These machines apply a resistance to muscle groups throughout the complete range of joint movement. The speed resistance and range can be also varied to meet the requirements of the injured limb. Although this type of equipment is expensive, research has shown that the results and recovery rate are far quicker than those achieved with conventional equipment. Unfortunately, the initial cost of this equipment makes it inhibiting to most centres. However, it is of great value in monitoring the progress of patients undergoing rehabilitation in any environment. If access to this type of equipment (e.g. Akron, Cybex or Nautilus) is available it can not only help the injured sportsman but also the therapist who can use it to both monitor and improve treatment regimes.

Motivation

Motivation can be of two kinds – external and internal. External motivation relates to factors outside of the patient's own psychological make-up that will encourage him to get better quickly, such as loss of earnings, pressures from managers/coaches/family, etc. and also the motivation given by the therapist treating that person. Internal motivation (or self-motivation) comes from within the patient's own personality and will help to determine the speed of recovery. If both types of motivation are low, then there will be little will to recover quickly. If the sportsman's self-motivation is low it is the job of the therapist and others to put some external pressure on him to balance the equation. Fortunately, most people who suffer a sports injury are highly self-motivated and anxious to return to their sport as quickly as possible. In this instance, the injured sportsman or his therapist may need to reduce the enthusiasm during activities so that they do not go too far. In this instance, the negative external motivation will balance the patient's increased self-motivation in order to achieve the best result.

Finally, if patients of similar backgrounds, injuries and interests are grouped

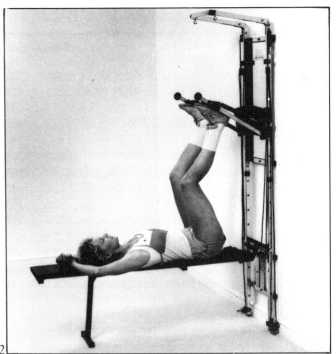

2

4

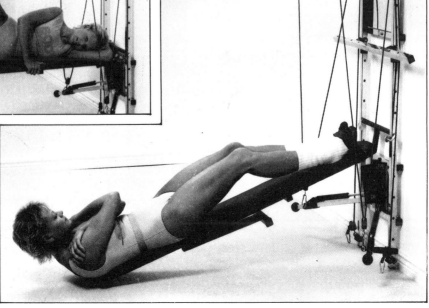

Weight training machines are often used in rehabilitation centres to strengthen muscles. Lat pull-downs to the back(1), the leg press (2), leg stretch (3) and sit-ups for the abdomen (4) show a range of exercises which can be performed with variable resistance from light to heavy.

together, they will also provide their own group motivation. This is the great advantage that rehabilitation at a sports centre provides. In a professional football club, a player carrying a long-term injury is often subconsciously ostracized from the main playing group by his injury, as he is unable to take part in all the normal activities that are involved within the club. Too often, the result is that the player becomes depressed and loses the will to recover quickly. If he attends a rehabilitation centre he will normally be part of a group, with players from other clubs suffering from similar disabilities and problems. He will then experience a sense of belonging within the group which will often be supportive to each member because all have experienced similar trials and tribulations at their own clubs. This sense of belonging naturally leads to increased motivation and the person's recovery rate should improve considerably.

Stages of rehabilitation

All rehabilitation should be divided into four main stages, regardless of the severity of the injury or the number of joints/muscles involved.

Stage 1 – Early rehabilitation

This stage includes the period of time where the limb is immobilised or the patient is non-weight bearing on crutches. All activities should be done so that full weight is not taken through any part of the injured limb at any time. With lower limb injuries, this means that all exercises or activities should be done while sitting. At no other time during this stage should competitive elements be introduced that might involve physical contact. It is, however, possible to play games while sitting, such as sit-down volley ball, sit-down cricket, etc. During this stage also, the unaffected parts of the body

can be worked hard, provided no adverse stresses or strains are placed upon the injured part. It is the therapist's responsibility to ensure that no 'risk' situations arise. For this reason, footballs should not be left lying around as the temptation to kick them will often be too great. Although the least active stage, it is often the hardest to control as both the injured sportsman and the therapist must be constantly aware of risk situations and the possibility of accidents occurring from the silliest of incidents.

Stage 2 – Intermediate rehabilitation

This stage encompasses the period from non-weight bearing through to the commencement of running. In lower limb injuries, it covers the period of non-weight bearing through partial weight bearing and finally full weight bearing. Re-training in walking should also be included during this period. Remember that this intermediate stage should only begin when joints can pass through at least two-thirds full range with no swelling or pain and the movement is a smooth, coordinated action without muscular 'judder'.

Stage 3 – Late rehabilitation

The most dynamic stage so far, when the patient will have all activities increased. There is more emphasis placed upon general fitness and activities in which the affected part is exercised without protection or limitations. Progress to this stage too early is often a major cause for re-injury or regression. It is, therefore, important that patients do not tackle this stage too quickly. It is far better to spend longer in the intermediate stage ensuring that the quality of work is good, rather than to rush through to the late stage before the sportsman is able to cope with the increased demands. It must be stressed once again that unless the walking pattern is correct, it will be impossible to run properly. Similarly, with all joint activities and gross movements (either lower or upper limb) the quality and coordination of the movements must be mechanically sound before the increased stresses and strains of the late stage are placed upon them. In many cases, this stage will be one of the shortest and should be a stepping stone to the final stage to come, rather than a high hurdle that, if not cleared comfortably, results in a fall-back to an earlier level. Therefore, careful assessment and realistic, unemotional decisions must be made before the sports-man embarks on late rehabilitation. If in doubt, don't.

Stage 4 – Pre-discharge

Often rehabilitation programmes stop when the patient is able to run. However, in sports rehabilitation, it is also important that be-sides being physically able to return to full activities, the patient is also psychologically prepared. Therefore, this stage should aim to achieve this, as well as allowing the therapist to confidently class the patient as 'fit'. The activities undertaken should include everything the patient is likely to do on his return to full, unrestricted training. In the case of footballers, this includes kicking, twisting, turning and all the other move-ments associated with that particular sport. Again, it is important that the therapist has some knowledge of the demands that are likely to be placed upon the patient when he returns to sport so that activities can be introduced that will place more stress upon the injured part than would occur during normal training programmes. The therapist should also be very optimistic and encourag-ing during this stage. Quite often, patients will be undertaking activities that caused the original injury and they may feel a certain apprehension and reluctance in case the injury 'breaks down'. The patient must be encouraged and helped over this 'hurdle' rather than pushed at, what is to him, a major barrier. If the sportsman has reached this stage too quickly and is not physically capable of completing the required tests, then the therapist can and will lose cred-ibility. It must, therefore, be stressed once again that this stage should not be under-

Gentle jogging is sometimes included in rehabili-tation programmes and you may even soon race again!

taken until the previous stages have been completed successfully. There are *no* short measures following injury to quicken the return to sport. If short cuts are taken, then injuries will recur, and not only will the sportsman's physical performance be af-fected, but their whole psychological make-up altered, too. An early return to sport without proper rehabilitation and prepar-ation usually means that original injuries recur and long-term problems increase. Successful completion of an appropriate 'pre-discharge' stage will completely mini-mise the risk of this happening.

Rehabilitation programmes

The following section outlines the main considerations applicable to the various parts and joints commonly injured and referred to a sports clinic for rehabilitation.

Ankle

Treatment of this joint should be divided into two main areas: range of movement and balance (proprioception).

The main ankle movements are plantar and dorsiflexion and inversion and eversion, i.e. pushing the foot down, up, in and out. As well as these active movements, there is also an important passive movement of this joint, too. If the foot is pulled back towards the leg as far as it will go, it will be noted that at the most, it is difficult to pull the foot past 90° at the ankle. However, when squatting with the heels remaining on the ground, the range of movement at the ankle is increased to over 120°. This functional passive movement must be present before running is resumed so exercises must be introduced which imitate this action and increase the range of passive 'dorsiflexion (see right). It is useful for the patient to compare the injured limb to the non-injured limb so that he can monitor his own progress and see any actual limitations of movement.

Balance at the ankle is as important as restoring movements. If it is not restored, then the risk of re-injury is extremely high. When normally standing on one foot, all balance reactions take place around the ankle without much conscious control. However, following injury, it often requires a much greater conscious effort to remain in this position because of altered balance. While running, you expect balance to occur naturally and do not consciously concentrate on it. It is only following injury that this reflex action is often painful when the ankle 'gives again'. To help restore balance, every day activities should be undertaken while standing on one foot, i.e. washing up, cleaning teeth, talking on the telephone,as well as exercises in a gym. This will restore it quite quickly, as will standing on uneven surfaces such as carpets, mats, trampettes and bouncing on small spring boards. Remember, however, that following any injury to the lower limb involving immobilisation of the ankle, balance must be tested and, if necessary, restored before any commencement of running.

To assess passive dorsiflexion: Hold raised foot flat, lean to bend ankle and compare with other leg.

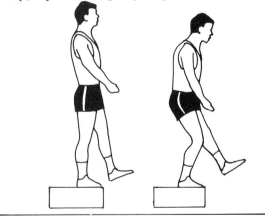

To increase passive dorsiflexion: Keep heel flat on step, step down using body weight to bend ankle.

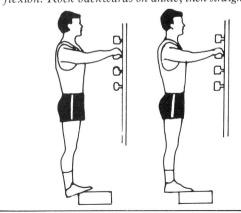

To strengthen calf muscles and increase passive dorsiflexion: Rock backwards on ankle, then straighten.

Knee

The knee is a highly complex joint, which with the increased knowledge available from the use of arthroscopes, seems to be getting more complicated. Along with the ankle, it is also one of the most likely joints to be injured in sport and to be seen in sports injury clinics. The mechanics and anatomy of this joint need to be studied and understood by anyone in sports injuries. Nowadays, it is not uncommon to find patients referred with cartilage or ligament injuries accompanied by anterior cruciate involvement – previously, it used to be cartilage or ligament or capsule injuries in isolation. Logically, the mechanics of this joint mean that it is nearly impossible to injure any one structure in isolation and both the sportsman and physiotherapist should be aware of this. When assessing this joint, do not stop because one structure has been affected, always look for an accompanying problem.

These quadriceps exercises are designed to strengthen and stabilise the knee joint. **1** *Bend leg on small roll at 15-45° angle, straighten, hold 5-10 seconds. Progress by repetition and increasing length of hold.*

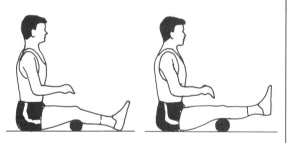

2 *Increase range of movement from 90° to full extension. Hold and progress as above. Add light weight boot to further strengthen.*

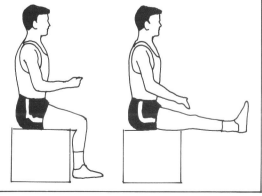

3 *Use body weight to move from sitting position to standing to sitting. Progress by lowering seat height.*

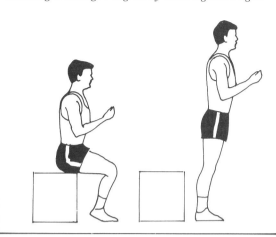

When planning any rehabilitation programme for this joint, it should be divided into knee injuries with anterior cruciate ligament involvement and injuries without. If there is no anterior cruciate involvement, the quadriceps (thigh) muscles are responsible for maintaining the stability and strength of the joint. Strengthening exercises, with the main concentration on strengthening the last 15-20° of extension, i.e. from a partial knee bend to a fully straight joint, are advised. Without the strength of this group of muscles, knee flexion will be limited. If a person attempts to bend the knee while the muscles are not strong enough to re-straighten it, the thigh muscles will go into a protective spasm that actually prevents any movement taking place – and if one tries to forcibly bend the knee through this spasm, the spasm will increase along with increasing pain in the knee joint. Once the strength of the quadriceps has improved and the knee can be straightened, then lightweight resistances can be added. A useful piece of equipment for this is a quadriceps bench.

A 'static quadriceps exercise' should be taught from day one following the injury and the patient advised and encouraged to do it whenever he or she consciously thinks about it. It simply involves bracing the thigh muscles tight with the knee straight and holding the contraction for as long as possible. A person can never do this exercise too often and it can be performed while sitting

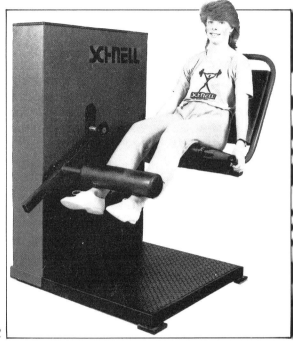

Among the range of machines for exercising muscle groups are the cam-operated system (1) and the leg extension machine (2) which automatically synchronises resistance.

on a bus, train, watching television or seated at work, etc.

If there is evidence of anterior cruciate ligament involvement in the injury, emphasis must be placed on strengthening the hamstring muscles at the back of the thigh ahead of the quadriceps. In the normal leg, the hamstrings should be 80 per cent of the quadriceps. However, in anterior cruciate ligament lesions, the hamstrings need to prevent the tibia (shin) and the femur (thigh) displacing and the knee giving way, especially during activities in which the knee is slightly bent and bodyweight taken through that leg. Hamstring strengthening exercises such as the ones opposite, should be introduced for patients with this type of injury.

Finally, there has to be a reciprocal co-ordination between the hamstrings and the quadriceps, so that knee flexion and extension becomes a smooth activity with no 'judder' or restriction at any stage of movement. Activities that involve rapid straightening and bending of this joint should be included. Walking forwards, backwards, up and down stairs, sitting to standing from a chair and cycling are all exercises that can be considered.

Hip joint

A ball and socket joint, the hip is able to pass through many ranges of movement. Even the action of walking, often considered so straightforward, involves rotational movements at the hip joint in both the supporting and moving leg. When assessing a hip joint injury, both hips should be compared. Any injury to this joint will give an altered walking/running pattern which, if not corrected, can become habit-forming and cause problems in other areas. If the patient has acute pain in the hip and walks with a pronounced limp, he should be on crutches (partial weight bearing) – there is little to be gained in being 'brave' and walking without assistance. An important point to remember is that 24 hours rest can often save weeks in correcting or rectifying problems that have been caused by a simple 'irritable' hip.

As well as increasing the range of hip movements following injury, the efficiency of the muscles acting around the joint must

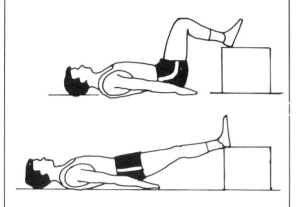

These exercises are designed to strengthen the hamstring muscles. **1** *Lie on floor with leg bent to step. Straighten legs, lifting buttocks. Hold 5-10 seconds. Relax and repeat.*

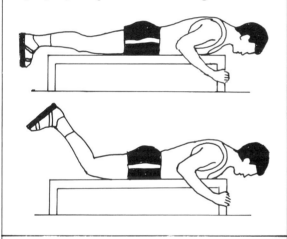

2 *Using light weight boot, raise leg from knee, hold 5-10 seconds. Repeat 20 times each leg or sequence of 25, 20, 15, 10 repetitions with each leg.*

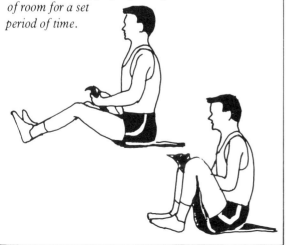

3 *Sit on blanket, digging heels into floor. Using heel and knee action, propel yourself around marked area of room for a set period of time.*

also be considered. Not only do these muscles have to be strengthened, but they should also have the ability to relax to allow opposite movements to take place. Too often following a hip/groin injury, the large adductor muscles (the muscles on the inside of the thigh) go into protective spasm as soon as the hips are stretched, in order to prevent this movement taking place. Therefore, if these muscles are not stretched adequately, when previous activities are attempted they will contract to prevent the movement. If this is followed too soon by some form of competitive sport, it is likely that they will be over-stretched and further injury incurred. A simple test to assess these movements is for the patient to lie on his back with both knees bent together and feet flat on the floor. When the knees are allowed to drop out to the side, both legs should fall out the same distance – with no tightness of the muscles to prevent the knees from being 'bounced' at the limit of the movement.

Both cycling and swimming will help problems that occur at this joint. However, it must be stressed again that it is not negative or over-cautious for patients with acute or painful hip joints to be rested for 24-48 hours in bed or on crutches before commencing any rehabilitation treatment.

Shoulder

As with the hip, this is a ball and socket type joint which has many ranges of movement, all accompanied with an element of rotation at the joint itself and within the shoulder girdle. Any injury of this joint, especially on the dominant limb, will result in a marked functional disability, especially with everyday activities. In the early stages of rehabilitation, concentration should be directed towards regaining ranges of movement, prior to strengthening. Simple pendular exercises are recommended such as standing bent forward so that the arm hangs perpendicularly towards the ground, then gently swinging it within the painful limits, to allow momentum to take the movement. This will help to increase and maintain the range of movement in the early days and prevent adhesions forming within the capsule. If not done, the result could be a 'frozen' shoulder

These shoulder exercises are aimed at regaining range of movement.
1 *Lean forward slightly and gently swing arm in circular arc, allowing momentum to initiate movement.*

2 *With stick or pole behind neck, raise hands above head, then lower onto chest. Raise above head and lower pole behind neck. Repeat, alternating chest and neck position.*

3 *Inching press-ups for strengthening fully mobile shoulder in late rehabilitation.*

syndrome, which is common in mistreated or older patients. Once the range of movement has improved, strengthening exercises using bodyweight or poles can be introduced. Other useful exercises specifically for the shoulder are shown opposite.

Elbow

Apart from tennis or golfer's elbow, (which are usually treated with local techniques) there are not many occasions other than fractures or dislocations where this joint is injured. However, when planning any form of rehabilitation for this joint, at no time should any elbow be forcibly straightened. Weights should also not be used on this joint if there is any limitation of movement. The reason for protecting the elbow in this manner is that all of the nerves and blood vessels that supply the hand pass over it. They also all lie anatomically in fairly vulnerable positions. Therefore, the golden rule is to never force any movement of the elbow. Movement *will* return to the joint in due course but under no circumstances should the patient try to extend the elbow by carrying heavy weights. Once the range of movement of the joint has returned, the main movements of flexion and extension can then be strengthened using lightweights with high repetitions.

Hand

The hand is a complex piece of machinery and it is only when any part of this structure is affected that one realises how much for granted its movements and actions are taken. When rehabilitating hand function following injury, a number of grips have to be restored.

Power grip Used for squeezing, as in holding a golf club, racquet or bat. Activities such as squeezing squash balls, putty, foam rubber, etc., can be done at home and work and also in a gym.

Pincer grip The fine precision movement involving the thumb, index and middle finger, used for picking up objects such as pens, pins, etc. Repetition is the best form of restoring this grip and even if it is the non-dominant hand (normally the left hand), the patient should use the hand regularly and not disregard it.

Key grip A sub-conscious action that everyone needs to pick up keys and put in doors. It involves holding the key with the thumb against a bent index finger and is usually an automatic grip. However, following injury, it is often difficult to perform. Again, repetition of the movement will restore the grip.

Baggage grip Used to carry bags with the ends of the fingers bent in to form a hook. Like the power grip, it can be restored by gripping and squeezing objects.

Only after the grips of the hand have been restored should sports activities be introduced. For racquet sports it may also be necessary to modify the size of the handle grips. Finally, when treating hand injuries, one must remember that the hand *is* a part of the arm and that without stability at the shoulder and elbow, the fixed structure required for hand movements will be affected. The arm, as a whole, must not be neglected and coordination of the whole limb should be re-educated using simple exercises such as catching, throwing, batting, etc. Even carpet bowls can be a useful and amusing activity for strengthening the whole limb.

Hamstrings and quadriceps

These two muscle groups, previously mentioned in relation to the knee joint, are both susceptible to serious injury in their own right. Also the increase in and the recurrences of hamstring injuries in top sports personalities has been highlighted in the media during the last few years. With any muscular injury, once the acute phase has passed, it is important that the mobility and flexibility of the muscle is restored, but this alone is not enough. No matter how quickly the acute injury is treated, there will always be a reduction in muscular strength. Therefore, both groups of muscles should be re-strengthened following any injury, no matter how minor. With recurrent hamstring injuries in many professional footballers it has been confirmed on Akron isokinetic equipment that the strength of the affected muscle is considerably weaker than that of the unaffected one. If the muscle is weaker, it will subsequently tire more quickly. Then, as with all injuries, protective muscle spasm will be induced to protect it. However, during competitive activities, the protective spasm will not prevent the dynamic forces being imposed upon the muscle and the fibres will be over-stretched and re-injury will occur. It is therefore very important that these muscles are strengthened to adequate levels before returning to any competitive sport.

Walking re-education

If a person cannot walk normally, any attempt to run will increase and magnify disabilities. Too often, patients 'give it a go' and try to run before they can walk without a limp. This will always lead to trouble. If the original injury is not exacerbated, then in modifying the action to protect the injury, other problems are likely to develop. Careful assessment of walking should be carried out before planning exercise regimes. A limp may be caused by limitation of movements at the foot, ankle, knee or even because of habit. Time must be spent in finding the cause and then eliminating it. Walking forwards, backwards and the use of mirrors will help to correct bad walking patterns. If there is a limp or an altered stride, this will be magnified as soon as running is attempted. If a patient walks for a couple of miles and experiences slight discomfort during the last half of the walk and noticeably limps, then if that same distance were to be run, the problems would worsen. Once gait has been corrected and the patient can walk without problems, the running stage will be easier and the rewards greater. This is an area that requires time, concentration and careful monitoring. However, if carefully handled, it will lay strong foundations for the later stages and eliminate the risks of secondary or primary re-injury. It is useful for the patient to monitor his own walking pattern and to vary the surfaces over which he walks, both indoors and outdoors.

Circuit training

Circuit training is another method of conditioning but with unique differences. It can be performed in a small space, indoors or outdoors at any time, using simple exercises with or without apparatus. It can be performed on an individual basis or in groups. There is nothing more boring or less appealing than doing the same circuit day after day to the same guidelines. Therefore, the therapist or the patient should regularly change the constraints and programmes while still retaining the efficiency and effectiveness of the exercises used. The usual method of circuit training is to perform a series of exercises to a fixed time, i.e., one minute work, 15-30 seconds rest, which although useful can be repetitive if done every session. However, as a first circuit, it is a useful method for assessing and recording the number of repetitions performed on each exercise but for training, the circuits and the format of timing should be modified.

Pairs (1 vs. 1)

Each member of the pair works for a fixed time on each exercise and records his total. The second member of the pair then does the same exercises for the same time and aims to beat the first. The person scoring the highest number of repetitions on that exercise wins the point. At the end of the circuit, e.g. 8 - 9 exercises, the one who has the highest number of points is the winner and the loser has to repeat the exercises for 10-15 seconds. This introduces a competitive element as well as giving a target to beat instead of waiting for the time to expire.

Pairs (2-man exercises)

For these circuits, each exercise has to be performed by both members of the pair at the same time, e.g. standing back to back with a ball between them and half-squats with the ball remaining in position. Each pair then tries to beat the score of the other pairs doing the exercise for the same fixed time – as in above, 8-9 exercises with a point to the winners of each exercise. The losers then re-do each exercise again.

Paired activity using a ball. Each pair must complete a fixed number of squats while retaining ball between their backs. These exercises may be modified by using larger/smaller or heavier/lighter balls. Progress by moving as a pair, across gym.

Variable timing (imposed by a member of the group)

During these circuits, one exercise acts as the timing for the remainder, e.g. shuttle runs, picking up 10 objects. The person undertaking this exercise determines the length of that particular activity for the rest. Therefore, the faster the task is completed, the less time is spent doing other exercises. The slower members are usually given 'gentle verbal encouragement' by the other members of the group to hurry up and complete the exercises so that they can stop doing the task that they are working on.

Fixed targets

Each exercise in the circuit is given a fixed target to complete, i.e. 30 press ups, 20 sit ups, 25 step ups. The members of the group have to complete the required number before moving on to the next exercise. A useful modification of this on a fixed station multi-gym is for the group to work around each station doing 25 exercises first circuit, 20 the second, 15 the third, and so on. They can work at their own pace and will gain more individual benefit than racing against the clock. It is a useful circuit to include when quality work is required.

Home circuits

Finally, it is important that patients have exercises that can be performed at home. The ingenious individual should be able to set up a home circuit to suit the needs of any patient so that the exercises can still be performed on days when there is no supervised treatment. Specific exercises, either to a fixed time or target, can usually be done with minimal disruption to domestic life.

In all aspects of circuit training, the work should be hard but modified in such a way that the patient has to think and concentrate rather than do a series of mindless exercises. Remember though, that the exercises must not be too complicated or dangerous.

Swimming

Not only is swimming a pleasant recreational activity, but it is also a means of working the whole body in a medium that gives both assistance and resistance to exercise. Hydrotherapy, using a pool for group or individual exercise treatments, can be advantageous in reducing recovery times, increasing range of movements and muscular strength. However, pools can also be used in the same way as a gymnasium for hard physical activity. Patients at rehabilitation centres usually have at least two sessions per week in a swimming pool. They are worked hard in the water for about one hour each session. Activities include relays, walking, treading water and retrieving objects from the bottom of the pool. Often they are the hardest

Swimming, which exercises the whole body, forms an important part of all rehabilitation programmes from initial stages through to late rehabilitation.

sessions that they experience – many professional footballers have confessed that they find pre-season training easier! Water sessions are used as an alternative to the circuit training and the gym for general fitness, as well as for specific individual exercises. Finally, water is a medium in which disabilities are equalised and patients in the early stages of rehabilitation are able to join in with those in the later stages, often competing on level terms. Any rehabilitation programme must include swimming, both for its psychological benefits and for the quality of work that can be achieved in the water.

Cycling is often used to achieve fitness in the intermediate stages of rehabilitation when running, which places stress on some muscles, would be inappropriate.

Cycling

Cycling can maintain and increase cardiovascular fitness during rehabilitation while patients are unable to run. A person has to be fit to run and cycling can be used as a means of achieving this fitness. Running also places stress on the ankle, knee, hip and back and during the period of intermediate rehabilitation, can exacerbate the original problems. Cycling, however, will allow the cardiovascular system to be worked hard while protecting these joints from the pounding received in running. A static bicycle can be used for general fitness work, although it can be boring to sit and pedal fervently while going nowhere in particular. Therefore, when planning programmes, include out-

door cycling around a track/circuit if possible. Besides working the cardiovascular system, cycling uphill is hard work for the quadriceps and hamstrings. This can be demonstrated on a static bicycle: using one leg only, and resting the other leg on a stool, cycle for a 10-minute period. After the activity the cycling leg will be noticeably tighter and larger in the quadriceps and calf than the rested leg. Therefore, this activity will maintain the strength of the unaffected limb even while the other limb is immobilised.

Once running is introduced into the late stage of rehabilitation, include cycling as well. The patients should cycle and run on alternate days for the first week before returning to full running every day.

Considerations for specific sports

Sports injuries need specialised care, not because they differ in an particular way from injuries sustained in the home or at work, but because the degree of stress involved in training or competition imposes stress on recently recovered tissues. They need longer periods of treatment because the level of fitness required is higher than for normal everyday life. Therapists and doctors should be as familiar with the athletic track, sports field or gymnasium as they are with their consulting rooms if they are to be really interested in rehabilitating sports injuries. They need to know all about the sport played by each patient and to be interested so that a close and understanding relationship can be developed. It is also useful for the sportsman to know what kind of treatments are particularly relevant to his sport.

Running/jogging

The current trend to get fit means that there is a wide variation in the levels of fitness of people who run or jog. The over-40 jogger who runs for basic fitness and the elite long-distance athlete who runs to compete at the highest level require their own level of functional fitness. Programmes, therefore, should be planned to meet the demands of each individual. An overweight 40-year-old cannot be expected to cover the same distance or produce the same work as a 60-mile-a-week cross country runner.

Twelve-minute fitness test

This test has been used for evaluating cardio-respiratory fitness of over 5,000 USAF personnel and is a suitable guide for general fitness. The individual runs/walks on a standard 400-metre track for 12 minutes. The following norms refer to the distance that should be covered during this time:

Distance	Fitness level
Less than 1 mile (4 laps)	Very poor
1-1¼ miles (5 laps)	Poor
1¼-1½ miles (6 laps)	Fair
1½-1¾ miles (7 laps)	Good
Over 1¾ miles	Excellent

Running over differing terrains will also improve cardiovascular fitness and muscular efficiency. Running downhill not only stengthens muscles but improves leg speed. Although running downhill places little stress on the lungs and heart, it is approximately 70 per cent more effective in strengthening muscles than running uphill for the same time. Leg speed can also be improved with high stepping while running. Although running is a fairly mundane activity that can become boring, programmes should be modified as much as possible to maintain interest and motivation.

Athletics

The actual demands required in athletics will depend upon the event competed in. In the pre-discharge stage it is, therefore, necessary for the athlete to work on technique as well as general fitness. Remember, too that the environment and atmosphere in which athletes compete can be stressful and rehabilitation treatment should encompass this aspect as well.

Football

Football is a physical contact game that

requires the ability to run, twist, turn, kick, tackle and be tackled. During a match, the players should be able to concentrate on the game rather than worry about fitness and/or re-injury. Too often players at every level return without proper training or rehabilitation. This is a recipe for disaster, which is not only morally wrong but could be classed as negligent when a doctor or therapist is involved. If a player cannot successfully complete training, then under no circumstances should he return to competitive matches. A game lasts for 90 minutes and it is not right to expect players who are only 80-90 per cent fit to play, simply because they

Footballers should always be tested to the limit before they are rated as fit. A premature return to competitive sport could result in re-injury.

will tire dramatically in the last 10 minutes of each half. They are then vulnerable to re-injury. Footballers should always be tested to the limit before they are classed as fit and placed back in the hands of managers/coaches/trainers.

Rugby

Rugby is an intensely physical game, requiring a high level of fitness. Every member of a rugby team must be able to pass a ball, catch a ball, tackle an opponent and be tackled. To achieve these skills, the players require a great degree of mobility, strength and coordination. Therefore before returning to training, they must be tested accordingly. There are also specific demands made

on certain positions which one must be aware of. The role of a hooker, for example, is far different from that of the scrum half and likewise, the centre has different needs to lock forward.

Rugby is also a game that requires 'explosive acceleration' from three basic starting positions – standing, lying and running. The impact of tackling, being tackled and striking the ground requires a higher level of fitness than is often found in other sports. Understanding and knowledge of this game is, therefore, a must for doctors or therapists treating rugby players.

Golf

Although considered a 'gentle sport', golf still requires a specific level of fitness – with the emphasis on mobility rather than endurance. To play 18 holes over undulating terrain requires a player who can not only walk long distances, but who is also able to carry a heavy bag of clubs. Note that golfers

Rugby requires considerable strength, mobility and co-ordination and any rehabilitation programme must aim at regaining these specific skills in an efficient way.

with any history of back pain should purchase a trolley. Spinal and shoulder mobility with correct posture are all necessary components of a good 'golf swing'. Any reduction in the range of movement of these areas will affect the swing and follow-through. Also, with the added momentum caused by the actual club, injury can often occur by taking the joints out of their pain-free range and re-injuring them. Even a mild chronic strain of an ankle or knee ligament can be exacerbated while playing golf, so golf is not a useful activity to substitute for other sports while recovering from injury. It is, however, an excellent sport to maintain spinal mobility but not to increase it. Bad habits learned by an injured golfer who insists on playing will often take months to iron out and this should (but does not always) stop a golfer playing when he is not fit enough.

Tennis, squash and badminton

These three racquet sports all require individual assessment and capabilities and very rarely does one find players who are exceptionally good at all three. Therefore, although grouped together, patients from each discipline must not be expected to have the same demands. Badminton requires players to dash forward, then run backwards. In the forward position, they crouch to play and at the back, they need to reach high for shots above their head. The badminton racquet action is from the wrist. Squash, however, is a dynamic sport played in a confined space. The player will remain in a semi-squat position throughout the match, placing both rotational and horizontal stresses upon both the knees and ankles. The racquet action for this sport is controlled from the elbow and forearm. Finally, tennis is played over a larger area and requires a greater degree of spinal and shoulder mobility to strike the ball. Where badminton and squash tend to be explosive sports over short distances, tennis requires a higher level of endurance.

Champion tennis players need a considerable degree of spinal and shoulder mobility.

Badminton requires strong wrist action, the ability to dash backwards and forwards and to reach high for shots.

Gymnastics

This is a physically demanding sport, in which the majority of participants are under 18. Not only do the problems that injuries cause have to be taken into account, but it is also necessary to be aware of the developmental problems that may occur. The disciplines can injure ankles, knees and backs and require strength, mobility and coordination to perform competently. Many gymnasts fall by the wayside because the sport constantly inflicts minor injuries. For top gymnasts, these are often ignored. Doctors and therapists involved with gymnasts should be aware of this – as should the gymnast – and should watch carefully for any alteration in walking, running or any guarding during landing. Certain common conditions, such as Osgood Schlatter's condition, (pain over the bony attachment of the quadriceps below the knee), twisted ankles and bruised knees will often respond to a short period of 5-10 days rest and this should be undertaken as a suitable treatment. There are many activities that gymnasts can still perform which will enable them to continue their training schedules while giving the lower limbs time to recover. Finally, this age group will undoubtedly suffer from 'growing pains'. These will usually last for only 24-48 hours and require no other treatment than sympathy unless they persist. Regular measurements of height will identify times that these are occuring or likely to be present.

Gymnasts frequently suffer minor injuries to ankles, knees and back which, if ignored, cause chronic problems.

Time, the great healer

Rehabilitation of sports injuries requires commitment, dedication and a willingness to learn by both doctor or therapist and patient and the effort required to treat patients will often be as hard as that provided by the patients themselves as they struggle to achieve their own goals. Each stage should be carefully observed and analysed so that modifications of programmes and progressions are justifiable and effective. Time can be a great healer and both therapist and patient should not be afraid to take time in assessment, monitoring and performing treatment programmes. Time can also be an enemy, which if one tries to beat, can cause all the good that has been done so far to be undone. Patients deserve and expect dedication, expertise and honesty from their medical advisors and there is no short cut to achieving or providing any of these. The demands are great, but the rewards are worthwhile. With forethought, imagination and commitment, the process of rehabilitation should be interesting and fun, not only for the patient but also for the therapists involved. Finally, the ultimate responsibility for recovery rests with the patients themselves. All that is provided by medical advice is the means to speed that process safely and effectively. No doctor or therapist will ever cure an injured sportsman, but rather give him the optimum conditions in which he can recover himself – until the next time!

CHAPTER SIX

DIET FOR INJURY PREVENTION

The relationships between nutrition and performance and performance and injury prevention are complex, but it is essential that the serious sportsman gives them some thought. Injuries are best prevented if the athlete competes and trains with the muscles prepared for work, not only by appropriate training, but also with the correct diet and fluid intake. Diet and fluid intake affect brain function as well as muscle activity, and vigilance and alertness are important in preventing injury, particularly in the fatigued. News stories of climbers slipping down the mountainside after some incredible physical achievement are all too familiar.

Importance of water

Dehydration is the chief enemy of good sports performance. Water forms a large proportion (approximately 60 per cent) of body weight. It is the essential medium to support the internal activities of tissue cells, to carry nutrients and oxygen around the body, amongst other things, to active muscles, to aid in the elimination of waste products and to get rid of excess body heat. These vital functions are less efficient if the body is dehydrated.

Normal body function depends on maintaining a fairly constant body temperature because the speed of the chemical (metabolic) processes varies with the temperature. So when a person exercises and produces more body heat, it is important that the extra heat is lost. When exercising at temperatures below that of the body, most heat (70 per cent) is lost into the atmosphere (radiation) by evaporation of sweat (27 per cent). As environmental temperatures get close to body temperature and as exercise increases, sweat evaporation contributes more to heat loss. Just how much sweat is lost depends upon the humidity of the environment, and so exercise in humid climates or conditions can lead to the dual problems of heat stress and dehydration. During sports activities in hot environments, sweat losses may be as much as 2-3 litres (4-5 pints) per hour. Air, wind and breezes affect the heat loss, as does the amount and type of clothing a person wears. About half of all sweat is lost from the thorax, one quarter from the arms and head, and the other quarter from the legs. Sweat which drips from the body does not help to regulate temperature, so athletes should choose clothing which absorbs sweat and allows it to evaporate and cool the body.

Effects of dehydration

During physical exercise, heat production increases and if body water lost by evaporation or dripping sweat is excessive, the result is dehydration. So if water is not available for perspiration, the body eventually overheats and neither the circulatory nor the temperature regulating systems of the body can cope with the demands and stresses of exercise.

The simplest way to measure dehydration

in an individual is by standardised weighing – i.e. weighing the individual accurately, preferably without clothes, before and after the sports activity. The weight loss corresponds to the amount of water lost. This can be calculated as a percentage of body weight. For example, if a person's weight before exercise is 9st 8lb (126lb/56.7kg) and after exercise is 9st 7lb (125lb/56.2kg), 1lb (450g) of water has been lost. This amounts to less than one per cent of body weight, a safe fluid loss for the sportsman. If, however, fluid loss is more than one per cent, the effects can be serious as this chart shows.

Effects of dehydration	
Weight loss as a % of body weight	Effect
1 – 3%	Impaired performance. Heat cramps may occur.
5%	Heat exhaustion – heart rate increases, the pulse is weak and rapid. Sweating profuse. Capacity for hard physical work decreases by 20-30%.
7%	Hallucinations occur.
10%	Heat stroke and circulatory collapse. Absence of sweating. Urgent medical attention required otherwise death follows.

Acclimatisation and physical conditioning

It takes about a week to become acclimatised to a hot climate. After this time, a person loses less sweat and also the salt content of sweat is reduced. Competitive athletes should make sure they have plenty of time to acclimatise to hot conditions. Physical training helps because it increases the blood volume and makes the sportsman less susceptible to the harmful reduction in blood volume that can occur in hard physical activity.

Replacement of water losses

The water lost during exercise is partly offset by the water produced when nutrients such as protein, carbohydrate and fat are metabolised to release energy. This is called metabolic water.

Carbohydrate is stored in the liver and muscles as glycogen together with water and potassium. When glycogen is broken down for energy, more water is released than just the metabolic water. An athlete who completely metabolises 500g (1lb) glycogen (2000 kcal) will gain 1.5 litres (2½ pints) of water which can partly compensate for fluid losses. However, the rest of the water needed must come from food and drink and it is surprising how much is present in some common foods.

Foods	% water
Wholemeal bread	40
Boiled potatoes	80
Boiled egg	75
Cheddar cheese	37
Grilled lean lamb chop	59
Roast chicken	68
Baked cod	77
Baked beans	74
Boiled cabbage	96
Peas	80
Tomatoes	93
Apple	84
Orange	86

Maintaining fluid levels

Anybody involved in active sport should ensure they are well hydrated before training or competition and every attempt should be made to maintain fluid intake during activity. Unfortunately, there is a limit to the

It is important to get adequate fluid during long-distance races. In big marathons, there are usually feeding stations (above) providing water and electrolyte drinks for consuming as you run (right).

amount of water we can replace – which depends on the speed at which the stomach empties. This, in turn, depends on the amount of liquid taken, the temperature of the liquid and the concentration of any other nutrients in the liquid. Generally speaking, large volumes are emptied more quickly but, during physical activity, they can cause discomfort and interfere with breathing. Up to 1 litre (1¾ pints) of fluid can be emptied in an hour and it is best taken in small frequent drinks of 150-200ml ($\frac{1}{4}$ – $\frac{1}{3}$ pint) every 10-15 minutes. Athletes should take water long before they feel thirsty, particularly when salts are being lost in sweat as well – merely quenching thirst itself does not supply enough water needs. Tennis players, for example, should always drink when they change ends between sets and marathon runners should start taking drinks early in the race.

Cold drinks empty more quickly from the

stomach and they can also contribute to keeping the body temperature low. Concentrated drinks of glucose and salts delay stomach emptying, so it is best if dilute solutions are used (about 5 per cent glucose). Remember, however, that it is more important for the active person to be properly hydrated than to take replacement glucose and salts.

Dehydration

As only about 1 litre (1¾ pints) of water loss can be replaced each hour, in endurance sports such as cross-country skiing, cycling and long-distance running, some dehydration is inevitable. These excess fluid losses should be replaced as soon as possible after the activity since it takes approximately 24 hours for fluid balance to be fully restored after serious dehydration.

Misunderstanding and abuse of body fluid balance

Where athletes compete in a weight class – for example, boxing, wrestling and rowing – there is a tradition of 'making weight' by losing body water. These athletes train at a weight above competition weight and use steam rooms, saunas, laxatives or diuretics to lose water just before weigh-in. Any time lapse between the weigh-in and match is usually spent trying to replace the lost fluid, which does not really help since fluid balance cannot be restored within 4-5 hours. This is not only foolish but dangerous and can result in some or all of the following consequences: reduction in muscle strength; decreased work performance; reduced heart function; poorer temperature regulation; depletion of liver glycogen stores and increased loss of vital salts.

An athlete's urine can be checked scientifically by examining its specific gravity with a hydrometer – if well hydrated, the specific gravity will be less than 1.015. A simpler, more accessible test for the amateur is to check the volume and colour of urine. A well-hydrated person produces a substantial flow of pale, straw-coloured urine at

Boxers and wrestlers (above) often achieve their target body weight for a competition by sweating off fluid, but this can be dangerous and may affect their health and performance in the ring.

least three or four times a day. Infrequent, small quantities of dark-coloured urine indicate dehydration.

Other causes of dehydration

Just as humid climates cause problems in the disposal of heat by evaporation, in very dry climates the atmosphere is not only dry but often less oxygenated. This is a particular problem at high altitude and also during long journeys by air, because the atmosphere in an aircraft is relatively dry. Consumption of alcoholic beverages increases dehydration and travelling sportsmen should take non-alcoholic beverages throughout the flight.

Vomiting and diarrhoea can also cause considerable fluid losses, so high standards of personal hygiene and care about what foods are eaten are wise precautions for the sportsman who travels widely.

Replacing salts losses

Sweat contains salts (or electrolytes) such as sodium, chloride, potassium and magnesium and, as exercise proceeds, the concentration of these in the blood tends to rise. For this reason, it is generally not advisable to take sodium and other salts during exercise, since the losses through sweat can quickly be replaced afterwards.

Fruit juice and instant coffee are rich in potassium, a little extra table salt in food can replace sodium and chloride losses and magnesium can be found in cereals and green leafy vegetables. In very hot humid weather and in long events, it may become necessary to replace some salts during the exercise. Many products with appropriate salt contents are available but it is most important to take one designed to be used during activity, rather than one designed to be taken after exercise has ended.

As shown in the table opposite, male cyclists require a very high calorie intake, followed closely by judo players, weight lifters and fencers who burn less energy.

Daily diet

The heavy physical activity of athletes in training and performance means they require a considerable amount of food to provide energy. Some examples of the calorie or energy intakes of Olympic athletes during training are given below.

	Male cyclists	Male fencers	Female fencers	Male judo players	Male weight lifters
Average energy intake (kilocalories)	4603	3218	2691	3752	3470
Range of	3174 - 7355	2314 - 4142	1807 - 4917	2462 - 5982	2459 - 4771

Appetite is a good guide to energy requirements and provided a wide range of foods is taken, vitamin and mineral needs will usually be met. A healthy diet for the sportsman should include a selection of food from each food group.

Meat group

Meat, poultry, fish, eggs, pulses

Dairy group

Milk, cheese, yoghurt

Fruit and vegetable group

Fruits, vegetables, fruit juices

Cereal group

Bread and cereals (whole-grain preferably)

Every day you should eat:

1 At least two portions from the meat group.
Portion sizes:
    100g (4oz) of meat or poultry
    175g (6oz) of fish
    2 eggs or 275-350g (10-12oz) of cooked pulses

2 Three portions from the dairy group.
Portion size:
    200ml (⅓pt) whole or skimmed milk.
    25g (1oz) cheese
    425g (15oz) yoghurt

3 At least four portions of vegetables and fruit.
Portion size:
    1 apple
    1 orange
    50g (2oz) green vegetables
    1 medium-sized potato

4 At least three portions of bread or cereals.
Portion size:
    2 slices of bread
    25g (1oz) cooked rice or pasta
    25g (1oz) breakfast cereal

Menu plans for active men and women

Example 1 (men)	**Calories**
Breakfast:	
2 poached eggs	147
100g (4oz) grilled bacon rashers	331
50g (2oz) grilled tomatoes	7
50g (2oz) grilled mushrooms	6
25g (1oz) cereal	105
3 slices toast	130
margarine	109
200ml (⅓pt) milk (skimmed)	62
Mid-morning:	
2 crispbreads	52
margarine	109
1 pear	61
Lunch:	
200g (7oz) vegetable soup	74
175g (6oz) haddock (steamed)	107
50g (2oz) carrots	11
50g (2oz) peas	23
4 medium boiled potatoes	320
parsley sauce 200ml (⅓pt) skimmed milk	62
10g (⅓oz) cornflour	33
1 baked apple	58
Mid-afternoon:	
200ml (⅓pt) skimmed milk	62
4 digestive buscuits (plain)	140
Dinner:	
2 × 100g (4oz) lean pork chops	512
2 medium baked potatoes	255
50g (2oz) sweetcorn	38
50g (2oz) runner beans	9
4 cream crackers	120
margarine (for crackers & potatoes)	292
Total calories:	**3295**

Example 2 (men) — Calories

Breakfast:

	Calories
½ grapefruit	26
25g (1oz) cereal	105
200ml (⅓pt) skimmed milk	62
2 boiled eggs	147
100g (4oz) grilled lean bacon rashers	331
2 slices toast	130
margarine	109

Mid-morning:

4 cream crackers	120
25g (1oz) cheese	115
margarine	109
1 apple	52

Lunch:

200g (7oz) mushroom soup	106
2 × 100g (4oz) lean chicken breast	322
4 medium boiled potatoes	320
50g (2oz) cauliflower	5
50g (2oz) carrots	11
1 banana	79
margarine on potatoes	109

Mid-afternoon:

200ml (⅓pt) skimmed milk	62
1 orange	52
2 wholewheat biscuits	70

Dinner:

2 × 100g (4oz) lean boiled gammon	379
100g (4oz) boiled rice	139
50g (2oz) broad beans	24
50g (2oz) cabbage	7
1 peach	37
4 crispbreads	104
margarine	219

Total calories: 3351

In field events where it is important to build muscle mass such as hammer throwing (above left) and pole-vaulting (left) where you need strength and explosive power, competitors usually eat a diet that is high in protein and low in fat and provides adequate calories for energy production.

Example 3 (women)   Calories

Breakfast:

½ grapefruit	26
25g (1oz) cereal	105
200ml (⅓pt) skimmed milk	26
2 slices toast	130
margarine	109
2 boiled eggs	147

Mid-morning:

2 crispbreads	52
margarine	109
1 apple	52

Lunch:

200g (7oz) mushroom soup	106
175g (6oz) baked cod	163
2 medium baked potatoes	255
50g (2oz) peas	23
50g (2oz) carrots	11
1 orange	52

Mid-afternoon:

2 slices toast	130
margarine	109

Dinner:

100g (4oz) lean boiled ham	136
3 medium boiled potatoes	240
50g (2oz) cauliflower	5
50g (2oz) broad beans	27
cheese sauce / 200ml (⅓pt) skimmed milk	62
25g (1oz) cheese	115
10g (⅓oz) cornflour	33
1 pear	41
4 cream crackers	120
margarine	146

Total calories: 2566

Lunch:

200g (7oz) tomato soup	110
100g (4oz) lean lamb chop (grilled)	252
3 medium boiled potatoes	240
50g (2oz) cabbage	7
50g (2oz) runner beans	9
1 peach	37

Mid-afternoon:

2 cream crackers	60
margarine	109
25g (1oz) cheese	115

Dinner:

100g (4oz) chicken breast	161
100g (4oz) boiled brown rice	139
50g (2oz) carrots	11
50g (2oz) cauliflower	5
1 apple	52
4 crispbreads	104
margarine	219

Total calories: 2521

Women athletes who want to build muscle need a low-fat, high-calorie diet of nutritious foods.

Example 4 (women)   Calories

Breakfast:

100g (4oz) grilled bacon rashers (lean)	331
50g (2oz) grilled tomatoes	7
50g (2oz) grilled mushrooms	65
2 slices toast	130
margarine	109
25g (1oz) cereal	105
200ml (⅓pt) skimmed milk	62

Mid-morning:

1 banana	79
200ml (⅓pt) skimmed milk	62

Do carbohydrates improve performance?

Nowadays most athletes eat only a light meal several hours before a race or competition, although they may increase their carbohydrate intake in the days leading up to the event itself.

There is a tradition among athletes, especially in so-called strength sports, of consuming large quantities of steak and other high-protein foods before an event but there is no evidence which suggests that this affects levels of performance. However, diets rich in carbohydrate and low in fat have been shown to improve performance of both long-term, low-intensity exercise and short-term, high-intensity exercise. High carbohydrate diets ensure that the liver and muscle glycogen stores are used up during exercise and high liver and muscle glycogen stores generally improve physical performance. However, it is important that liver glycogen stores are full before exercise begins because the liver is an important source of glucose for brain function and helps maintain blood glucose levels. Research in other fields supports this. Accident rates, for example, were lower amongst forge workers who took a glucose drink, and glucose drinks have also been shown to improve driving performance on a automobile simulator. Alertness and reaction time are important both in preventing injury and in improving sporting performance, and maintenance of glycogen reserves before exercise and taking glucose drinks during long duration exercise may well help to prevent injury.

Weight control

Being overweight can put additional strain on muscles, joints and cartilages leading to injury. Usually as athletes train, the size of muscles increases and the body's fat content decreases. However, there are occasions, particularly after a rest period, when sportsmen may well want to reduce their weight, although it must be emphasised that harsh slimming regimes, which can mean loss of muscle tissue as well as fat, should be avoided.

Body fat weighing 450g (1lb) is roughly equivalent to 3500 kilocalories, so in order to lose 900g (2lb) weight in a week the daily energy or calorie intake has to be 1000 kilocalories less than the energy used up. For the average male athlete training two hours a day, the energy intake should be reduced to around 2300 kilocalories and for the average female athlete in training, 1500 kilocalories a day.

The reduced calorie menus show it is possible to lower energy intake without too much effort and one of the best ways is to eat less fat because fat is the most concentrated form of energy. See the tips below on ways to reduce fat intake.

Hints for reducing fat intake

- Remove visible fat from meat.
- Eat smaller portions of meat.
- Substitute chicken and fish for red meat.
- Remove the skin from chicken.
- Grill, boil, steam or braise food rather than frying.
- Substitute low-fat spreads for butter and margarines or use less butter and margarine.
- Substitute cottage cheese or low-fat cheeses for hard cheeses with a high-fat content, such as Cheddar.
- Replace mayonnaise dressings with natural yoghurt.
- Replace whole milk with skimmed milk.

Women athletes who need to reduce fat content in their bodies but not at the expense of muscle tissue should eat low-calorie, nutrient-dense foods.

Weight reducing diets of less than 1500 kilocalories rarely supply all the essential nutrients the athlete needs but if a very low calorie diet has to be followed, it is advisable to take a well-formulated nutritional supplement. The Microdiet and Cambridge diets which contain all essential nutrients provide an excellent basis for a more liberal weight reducing regime.

Needless to say, it is vitally important that weight is never controlled by dehydration; to do so can have disastrous effects on performance and increase the risk of sports injury.

Reduced calorie menu plan

Example 1 (Men)	Calories
Breakfast:	
2 boiled eggs	147
25g (1oz) cereal	105
2 slices toast	130
margarine	109.5
200ml (⅓pt) skimmed milk	62.5
Mid-morning:	
2 crispbreads	52
margarine	109.5
Lunch:	
50g (2oz) vegetable soup	74
175g (6oz) steamed haddock	167
50g (2oz) carrots	11
50g (2oz) peas	23
4 medium boiled potatoes	320
parsley sauce / 200ml (⅓pt) skimmed milk	62.5
10g (⅓oz) cornflour	33
1 apple	52.5
Mid-afternoon:	
200ml (⅓pt) skimmed milk	62.5
1 peach	37
Dinner:	
100g (4oz) lean pork chop	256
2 medium baked potatoes	255
50g (2oz) sweetcorn	38
50g (2oz) runner beans	9.5
2 cream crackers	60
margarine	109.5
Total calories:	**2586**

It is easy to lose weight through dehydration when training and racing in hot weather but this can be dangerous. Take plenty of liquids to replace lost fluids.

Example 2 (Men)

	Calories
Breakfast:	
½ grapefruit	26
25g (1oz) cereal	105
200ml (⅓pt) skimmed milk	62.5
2 boiled eggs	147
2 slices toast	130
margarine	109.5
Mid-morning:	
2 cream crackers	60
25g (1oz) cheese	115
margarine	73
Lunch:	
200g (7oz) mushroom soup	106
100g (4oz) lean chicken breast	161
4 medium boiled potatoes	320
100g (2oz) cauliflower	5
100g (2oz) carrots	11
1 banana	79
Mid-afternoon:	
200ml (⅓pt) skimmed milk	62.5
1 orange	52.5
Dinner:	
100g (4oz) lean boiled gammon	189.5
100g (4oz) boiled rice	139
50g (2oz) broad beans	24
50g (2oz) cabbage	7.5
1 peach	37
4 crispbreads	104
margarine	219
Total calories:	**2345**

Whatever sport you practise, whether it's running, hurdling, gymnastics or long jump, you must ensure that your diet provides adequate nutrients and calories for health maintenance and injury prevention. Women athletes in particular must get sufficient iron in their diet, and beware of restricting their calorie intake to the point where there is a danger of becoming anorexic.

Example 3 (Women)	Calories
Breakfast:	
½ grapefruit	26
25g (1oz) cereal	105
200ml (⅓pt) skimmed milk	62.5
2 slices toast	130
low fat spread	55
Mid-morning:	
1 apple	52.5
Lunch:	
175g (6oz) baked cod	163
2 medium baked potatoes	255
50g (2oz) peas	23
50g (20z) carrots	11
1 orange	52.5
Mid-afternoon:	
1 pear	41
Dinner:	
100g (4oz) lean boiled ham	136
2 medium boiled potatoes	160
100g (2oz) cauliflower	5
50g (2oz) broad beans	27
cheese sauce / 200ml (⅓pt) skimmed milk	62.5
25g (1oz) cheese	115
10g (⅓oz) cornflour	33
1 pear	41
Total calories:	**1556**

Example 4 (Women)	Calories
Breakfast:	
25g (1oz) cereal	105
200ml (⅓pt) skimmed milk	62.5
2 slices toast	130
low fat spread	55
Mid-morning:	
200ml (⅓pt) skimmed milk	62.5
Lunch:	
200g (7oz) tomato soup	110
100g (4oz) grilled lean lamb chop	252
2 medium boiled potatoes	160
50g (2oz) cabbage	7
50g (2oz) runner beans	9.5
Mid-afternoon:	
25g (1oz) cottage cheese	27
2 crispbreads	52
low fat spread	55
Dinner:	
100g (4oz) chicken breast	161
100g (4oz) boiled brown rice	139.5
50g (2oz) carrots	11
50g (2oz) cauliflower	5
1 banana	79
Total calories:	**1520**

SPORTS INJURY CLINICS IN THE UK

Here is a list of NHS and private sports injury clinics in Great Britain, as at the date of first publication. The list is not comprehensive and your doctor or local sports centre may be able to recommend others.

NHS clinics

These clinics will treat you free of charge but may require a doctor's referral letter. It is advisable to check with these hospitals on details of referral, waiting time for an appointment and whether you have to live within the catchment area.

Greater London

Hackney Hospital
Homerton High St
London E9
Tel: 01-985 5555

The London Hospital
Whitechapel
London E1
Tel: 01-377 7000

Mayday Hospital
Mayday Rd
Thornton Heath
Croydon
Surrey
Tel: 01-684 6999

Medical Rehabilitation Centre
152 Camden Rd
London NW1
Tel: 01-485 1124

The Middlesex Hospital
Mortimer St
London W1
Tel: 01-636 8333

Royal Northern Hospital
Holloway Rd
London N7
Tel: 01-272 7777

St Bartholomews Hospital
West Smithfield
London EC1
Tel: 01-600 9000

St Charles Hospital
Exmoor St
London W10
Tel: 01-969 2488

Westminster Hospital
Horseferry Rd
London SW1
Tel: 01-828 9811

Outside London

Aldershot: Cambridge Military Hospital
Aldershot
Tel: (0252) 22521 ext. 208

Bedford General Hospital
Kempston Rd
Bedford
Tel: (0234) 55122

Birmingham Accident Hospital & Rehabilitation Centre
Bath Row
Birmingham
Tel: 021-643 7041

Birmingham General Hospital
Steelhouse Lane
Birmingham
Tel: 021-236 8611

East Birmingham Hospital
Bordesley Green East
Birmingham
Tel: 021-772 4311

Cambridge: Addenbrookes Hospital
Hills Rd
Cambridge
Tel: (0223) 45151

Cuckfield Hospital
Haywards Heath
Sussex
Tel: (0444) 459122

Derbyshire Royal Infirmary
London Rd
Derby
Tel: (0332) 47141

Glasgow: Victoria Infirmary
Glasgow
Tel: 041-649 4545

Guildford: St Luke's Hospital
Warren Rd
Guildford
Tel: (0483) 71122

Hereford General Hospital
Nelson St
Hereford
Tel: (0432) 272561

Hillingdon Hospital
Hillingdon
Uxbridge
Tel: (0895) 38282

Liverpool: Newsham General Hospital
Belmont Rd
Liverpool
Tel: 051-263 7381

Northampton General Hospital
Northampton
Tel: (0604) 34700

Oswestry Institute of Orthopaedics
Oswestry
Shropshire
Tel: (0691) 655311

Oxford: Nuffield Orthopaedic
Centre
Oxford

Tel: (0865) 64811

Plymouth: Freedom Fields
Hospital
Greenback
Plymouth

Tel: (0752) 668080

Sun afternoon from 2pm by
appointment only. Conducted
voluntarily.

Portsmouth: Soft Tissue Injury
Clinic
St Mary's General Hospital
Portsmouth

Tel: (0705) 822331

Southampton General Hospital
Shirley
Southampton

Tel: (0703) 777222

Wexham Park Hospital
Wexham
Slough
Bucks

Tel: (75) 34567

Weymouth & District Hospital
Melcombe Ave
Weymouth
Dorset

Tel: (03057) 72211

Private physiotherapy clinics

The clinics listed below all employ
chartered physiotherapists but have
no doctors in attendance. They are
all open to members of the general
public. RNR indicates that a referral
letter is not required and RNR*
that although a referral letter is not
required your GP will be informed
by the clinic that you have received
treatment there. Details of chartered
physiotherapists, in your area, with
an interest in sports medicine can
be obtained by writing with an SAE
to Brian Webster, Secretary,
Association of Chartered Physiotherapists in Sports Medicine, 14
Mayfield Court, Mayfield Road,
Moseley, Birmingham B13 9HS

Blackpool: Fylde Coast Hospital
St Walburgas Rd
Blackpool

Tel: (0253) 34188

Tue and Thur 9am-4pm by
appointment only (weekends may
soon be possible) RNR*.

Bushey: Hartspring Sports &
Leisure Centre
Park Avenue
Bushey
Watford
Herts

Tel: (92) 33039

Tue 6.30-8.30pm; RNR*.

Bristol: JH Sports Injuries Clinic
158a Church Rd
(Baines St entrance)
Redfield
Bristol

Tel: (0272) 550806

Mon, Tue, Wed and Thur
9.30am-4.30pm, Fri 9.30am-
1.00pm, Sun 10am-1pm; Tues and
Thur 6pm and 8.30pm; RNR*.

Derby: Derbyshire Sports Injuries
Clinic
The Lund Pavilion
Derbyshire County Cricket Club
The County Ground
Nottingham Rd
Derby DE2 6DA

Tel: (0332) 369 713

Mon 7-8pm. No appointment
necessary; RNR.

Eastbourne: Sports Physiotherapy
Clinic
Dittons End
Southfields Rd
Eastbourne

Tel: (0323) 25300

Almost any time by appointment
only; RNR.

Edinburgh: The Sports Centre
Heriot Watt University
Riccarton Campus
Currie
Midlothian

Tel: (031) 449 5111

Mon-Fri by appointment only.
University sports facilities also open
to general public if used as part of
treatment.

Hemel Hempstead: Dacorum
Sports Centre
Park Rd
Hemel Hempstead
Herts

Tel: (0442) 64822

Mon 6-9pm, Wed 6-8pm, Fri 12-
2pm; RNR.

Hornchurch: Sports Injury Clinic
Hornchurch Swimming Pool
Hornchurch
Essex

Tel: (45) 46995

Mon, Wed and Fri 6.30pm-
8.30pm; RNR*.

Leatherhead Leisure Centre
Guildford Rd
Leatherhead
Surrey

Tel: (0372) 377674

Tue and Thurs 6-8.30pm; RNR*.

Letchworth: North Herts Leisure
Centre
Baldock Rd
Letchworth

Tel: (0462) 679311

Wed 5.30-8pm; RNR*.

Manchester: Heaton Park
Physiotherapy Clinic
121 Bury Old Rd
Prestwick
Manchester

Tel: 061-773 1508

Mon-Fri 8.30am-7pm; RNR.

Marlow: Bisham Abbey National
Sports Centre
Marlow
Bucks

Tel: (06284) 76911

Mon and Thurs 6-8pm; RM

Preston: Fulwood Leisure Centre
Black Bull Lane
Fulwood
Preston

Tel: (0772) 716085

Mon and Thur 6-8pm; RNR.

Tonbridge: Angel Centre
Angel Lane
Tonbridge
Kent

Tel: (0732) 359966

Mon and Thurs 7-9pm; RNR*.

Truro: Duchy Hospital Sports
Clinic

Tel: (0872) 70068

Mon-Fri 5.30-9pm, Sat and Sun
9-12 noon; RNR*.

INDEX

All numerals in *italics* refer to illustrations.

Acknowledgements

Photographs
We would like to thank the following photographers, companies and individuals for supplying photographs used in this book:

All-Sport Photographic Ltd: cover
Bolton Stirland International Ltd: page 105
David: page 114
International Sport and Leisure Marketing Ltd: page 109
Le Coq Sportif: pages 14, 15
Powersport: page 107
Royal National Orthopaedic Hospital: pages 37, 38, 41, 46, 47, 50, 53, 64, 69, 75, 81
Schnell UK Ltd: page 114
Mark Shearman: pages 9, 10, 11, 12, 13, 19, 20, 21, 45, 85, 111, 119, 120, 122, 123, 124, 125, 128, 129, 130, 131, 133, 134, 135, 136, 137, 138, 139
Spenco: pages 16, 86, 92
Graham Smith: page 106
Brian Webster: pages 95, 97, 99, 100

Illustrations
Our thanks to International Sport and Leisure Marketing Ltd for permission to reproduce the artwork illustrations for flexibility exercises and the male muscular and skeletal system featured on pages 26, 27, 28, 29, 30, 31 and 35.

Also to Al Rockall for all the anatomical illustrations in *The Sports Body* chapter.